How to Mount Aconcagua

A Mostly Serious Guide to
Climbing the Tallest
Mountain Outside the
Himalayas

Jim Hodgson

ISBN: **1490412573**
ISBN-13: **978-1490412573**

DEDICATION

This book is dedicated to my grandfather, Robert William Bryant. His shotgun and his watch are both now mine. I hope someday his quiet strength will be as well.

I miss you, Grandpa.

CONTENTS

NAMES

I have changed everyone's names in this account because using real names is a legal no-no, even if you say nice things about the names you include. Such is the world in which we live.

HOW TO MOUNT ACONCAGUA

1 WHY ACONCAGUA?

Geography lies. For example, a continent is defined by Webster's dictionary as "...great divisions of land on the globe," and there are seven of them: Asia, Europe, Australia, North America, South America, Africa, and Antarctica. But geographers and scientists say there are only six continents, because calling Europe and Asia separate just because mountains run between them is like a married man calling himself single merely because he's sick of his wife. Let's face it, though—Europe can be like that sometimes.

As long as we're getting technical, North America and South America were also a continuous expanse of land until a French diplomat named Ferdinand de Lesseps came along in 1881 and began digging a canal across the thinnest part, called an "isthmus." De Lesseps was flush with success, having recently dug the Suez Canal in Egypt, and spirits were high. The idea of the Panama project had been floating around for quite some time—even advocated by Benjamin Franklin and Thomas Jefferson—but the French project sputtered and failed. Nearly 100 years later, the

United States assumed and completed work on the Panama Canal, taking much of that time to compose palindromes about it.

I explain this about the continents because mountaineers, in defiance of their geographer and scientist counterparts, agree that there are seven continents, even though a strong case could be made for six, or even five. They do this thanks partly to a man named Richard Bass, who was born in an ancient time (1929) when being called "Dick" was not a judgment of any kind on one's demeanor. Bass, himself a Yale University geology graduate, opened a ski resort in 1971. The resort prospered. According to an oft-repeated but ill-cited quote from Bass, that prosperity was due to his own "blanket curiosity, nonstop verbosity, and hyperenthusiasm."

"I'm thinking about going skiing today," one of his resort guests may very well have said.

"You'd better damn well get out there and ski like your life depends on it! Rarrrgh!" Dick Bass may very well have exclaimed, leaping onto a nearby table and hyperenthusiastically tearing open his shirt.

Prosperous and enthusiastic Dick Bass, along with his buddy Frank Wells, who was himself a prosperous president of Warner Brothers Studios at the time, concocted a plan to summit the highest peaks on each of the seven continents. According to their book about the adventure, The Seven Summits, Bass had the idea to climb all seven peaks while descending Alaska's Denali after a successful summit.

Actually, in The Seven Summits, Bass called the mountain by its more commonly known name, "Mount McKinley," which it acquired when miner William Dickey wrote a newspaper article in the New York Sun describing how he "discovered" the peak in 1897. He chose the name McKinley after then-presidential-hopeful William McKinley of Ohio. Dickey chose this name for no reason other than he was himself a conservative who wanted

McKinley to win. I don't personally have any mountains, but I wonder how I would like it if someone came along and renamed one of my little nieces after some presidential candidate. Dickey was not at all bothered that presidential hopeful McKinley never even set foot in Alaska in his life, let alone laid eyes on Denali. Also problematic is that the mountain had already long since been discovered centuries ago by the native Alaskans who lived nearby. They called it "Denali," which means "the high one" in their language. Things get a bit complicated from there, because McKinley was shot and killed in Buffalo in 1901 while president. That's a tragedy in anyone's book, one that should be remembered forever—just not as a mountain's name.

Even now, in the year 2013, Alaskans such as Sen. Lisa Murkowski, R-AK, are fighting Ohioans over the right to let their mountain go back to the name it had before white people showed up and started "discovering" things natives already knew about. Congressman Ralph Regula, R-OH, led opposition to the name change until he retired in 2009, but the pressure to keep Denali McKinley is still alive and well. Recently, Rep. Tim Ryan, D-OH, said that the name McKinley must be retained "in order to honor the legacy of this great American President and patriot." Of course, Rep. Ryan is right that we should remember the legacy of President McKinley. He was, after all, our 25th president, which I believe makes him the silver president, but is he really in any danger of being forgotten? I mean, he did lead the United States to victory in the Spanish-American war. He did get elected president. It's not as though having his name slapped on Denali is the only thing keeping his memory alive. In fact, I think keeping his name on Denali is pretty dumb, so I call that particular mountain Denali.

Richard Bass and Frank Wells weren't troubled by any of these disputes, however, living as they were in the halcyon days of the early 1980s. Their list of seven summits included Kosciuszko (2228 meters) in Australia, Elbrus (5,642 meters) in Russia, Vinson Massif (4,892 meters) in Antarctica, Everest (8,848 meters) in Nepal and China, Denali (6,194 meters) in the United States, Kilimanjaro (5,895 meters) in Tanzania, and Aconcagua (6961 meters) in Argentina.

There is another list, called the Messner list after its creator, famed alpinist Reinhold Messner. An "alpinist" is another word for mountaineer, and Messner is certainly one of those. In 1980 he was the first to summit Everest without the use of supplementary oxygen. The Independent, a newspaper in the United Kingdom, called him "the greatest climber in history" in 2006. He's climbed everything worth climbing, and was the first to summit many of the world's highest peaks. He's crossed deserts, trekked across Greenland, and spent time tracking the yeti, or abominable snowman. He even claims to have seen a yeti in his book, My Quest for the Yeti, though he was not able to produce any solid proof of the encounter. Yetis aside, he's unquestionably a mountaineer's mountaineer.

The Messner list includes the Carstensz Pyramid (4,884m) in Indonesia instead of Kosciuszko. Messner felt that the Carstensz Pyramid should be on the list instead of Kosciuszko simply because it is taller. To get to the top, a climber has to actually climb, whereas summiting Kosciuszko, with its very low altitude and nicely paved path to the top, is within the capabilities of a determined house cat. Still, Bass and Wells preferred the slightly more geographically correct Kosciuszko.

I should say at this point that I will be expressing height in meters because that's how it's done in mountaineering. If you want to convert to feet, multiply the meters by 3.3, or 3.2808399 if you want to be super technical about it. Realize, however, that if you must make any conversion from metric to imperial units and there are people from countries other than America around, they are likely to huff at you. For example, a few days into our trip I wondered aloud what the temperature would be at the summit. "Negative tree or four," responded Irishman

Darragh, fellow climbing party member. He was a professional guide himself, climbing Aconcagua on vacation from his usual gig in the Alps. Apparently, years ago, Darragh left the military and decided that civilian life wasn't for him, so he set about trying to keep clients from tumbling off Europe's peaks instead.

"Three or four C?" I asked. "What's that in F?"

"Fookin Americans," he responded.

My friend Mark and I climbed Kilimanjaro together in 2010 via the Lemosho route. That trip remains far and away the most enjoyment I have ever received for dollars spent in my life. Since we enjoyed Kili so much — once you've summited a mountain you're allowed to address it by a nickname — and since it's on both the Bass and Messner lists, we thought we might like to try another of the seven: Aconcagua. It has many similar qualities to Kilimanjaro without being nearly as expensive, time-consuming, or lethal as some of the more challenging peaks.

All of the other summits have troublesome challenges. For example, Denali is known to be very, very cold. Climbers who attempt to summit Denali wear 50- to 60-pound packs in addition to a 30-pound sled that they drag behind themselves. I say Rudolph the red-nosed no thanks. Elbrus is in Russia, and while it isn't very tall, I am told that the support structure for climbing parties is iffy at best. I've also heard that they have some very enthusiastic local gangs. Everest is prohibitively expensive and time-consuming. Expeditions can run upwards of $60,000 and can take months, plus climbers are in constant danger of being shoved off the mountain by a yak. I am not making that up about the yaks, by the way. Vinson Massif isn't terribly tall, but it is in the middle of Antarctica, which is our planet's impenetrable icy underpants. The Carstensz Pyramid requires a lot of ropes and scrambling over jagged rocks. Sounds to me like a great way to skin a knee.

Aconcagua, on the other hand, is high, but non-technical. When I use the term "technical," it is to denote the use of equipment and techniques which require skills to safely employ. Skills, to be perfectly honest, that Mark and I did not have at the time. Aconcagua is also located in Argentina, in the Andes mountain range, which was formed as the South American Tectonic Plate shifted into the Pacific Plate. Situated as it is in Argentina, it is very close to the famous wine-drinking and beef-chorizo-eating city of Mendoza. Good luck getting yourself a decent latte in Antarctica or the high Himalayas, let alone a delicious Malbec. I mean, we're interested in adventure, but there are limits.

Thus, the choice was made. Aconcagua it would be. We decided too late for the nearest climbing season, though, in the fall of 2011, so we had to wait a full year until December 2012 to set off. In that time we read books, web pages, and message boards and used the knowledge gained there to purchase a truly staggering amount of cold weather gear. We also "trained" for the climb. I use quotes because while we did walk many times up local mountains with weighted packs on our backs, physical effort at sea level and at altitude are very different propositions. Our home in Atlanta, Georgia has two mountains close by, Kennesaw Mountain (551 meters) and Stone Mountain (251 meters), but if either were in the Andes near Aconcagua they would surely not have names. They'd just be "that hill over there" and "that other one." Still, we walked up and down Kennesaw and Stone Mountain quite a lot with weighted packs and pouring sweat.

Fitness is important, but altitude sickness is the biggest obstacle facing any would-be Aconcagua climber. It is impossible to predict how severe altitude sickness will be from person to person, or even from trip to trip for the same person. It's kind of like being in a room with a very temperamental yeti. It might take a nap, or it might leap on you and tear you to ribbons. There's no way to know until it's too late.

Now you know some hard details about why we chose Aconcagua, but why, in a philosophical sense, would anyone want to go to high altitude in the first place? Why do any of this? Aconcagua is tall and there's very little oxygen at the top of it. It's a lot of work. Maybe too much, but then, a lot of things are hard. Being alone is hard. Losing someone is hard. What am I going to think with my last thought, I wonder? Will it be something like "Oh shit, this is it," or something self-conscious like "Augh! My socks don't match and the EMTs are judging me"? If I'm honest, it'll probably be more like "I wish I'd done more." When I think about life ending, I think it might be a lot like leaving a party early.

I am lucky. My legs work. My lungs work. Don't I have a duty,

given that I have those resources, to use them? Don't I have a duty to the people who are no longer with us to run as far and climb as high as I can? I think so. I mean, like I said before, there are limits. I tend to stay away from some more dangerous pastimes, even though they are seriously fun, because I know that I will go wrong at some point. I have good balance, but going wrong is a statistical eventuality in my view. That's why I have to be careful not to spend too much time on motorcycles. It's a shame, because they are pretty much the most fun things ever, but I've got a number of permanent injuries just from bicycle wrecks. I can't ride a bike anywhere nearly as fast as I can drive a motorcycle. You won't catch me base jumping or in a wingsuit either, though I'm sure those activities are mind-blowing.

Being uncomfortable on a mountain has benefits. It puts daily life into perspective. I look around at my nice warm apartment with the sun angling through the blinds and I feel lucky to be here. Would I ever have that thought if I didn't spend at least a little time each year being profoundly uncomfortable? I think probably not. Mind you, Aconcagua is not the tallest or the toughest mountain in the world. It isn't very technical, either, but then, I am not a mountaineer. I am a writer who likes going outside and then making jokes about it.

2 DAY ONE

A van carried us from our hotel in Penitentes, ski resort and nearest town to Aconcagua, to the park. The resort was a bit strange, although staffed by some very kind people. It had a bit of a "The Shining" feel to it, architecturally, but it was comfortable enough. We'd divided our gear up into two duffel bags: one to be taken by the mules to base camp, and the other to stay closer to us. We divided up our gear like this because a lot of it isn't necessary until we reach the higher camps, so it might as well get trundled up to base camp on a mule train.

A few of the guys weighed themselves for comparison purposes, planning to step on the scales again when we returned from the mountain to see how much weight they'd lost. I was so busy fretting over what gear to put in which duffel bag I missed this little ritual.

At the park, our head guide Sebastian, or "Seb" for short, handled some transactions with the park rangers helped by second guide Nicolas, or "Nico." We'd gone through some confusing money changing and permit purchasing back in Mendoza to obtain the privilege of entering. This process required us to exchange $700 or so into Argentinian pesos. It's a lot cheaper to enter the park early or late in the season, but then you're more likely to freeze your butt off.

At the park's entrance, the wind gusted quite enthusiastically, perhaps even reaching Dick Bass levels. We could see the white peak of Aconcagua from the parking lot. It looked closer than two weeks away, like we could just trot to the top and be back for beef chorizo and Malbecs by nightfall. The speed record for a summit attempt is said to be less than a day, but no good records are kept and there's a lot of arguing about who has proof of what. Rest assured, it took us much longer than a day.

Once we'd unloaded the van and shouldered our packs, we set off. I found myself walking next to Darragh the Irish mountain guide, and chatted a bit with him about the trip ahead.

"So," he said to me, as we crossed the Horcones River on the first trekking day. We were walking, incidentally, on a suspension bridge that was built for the Brad Pitt movie "Seven Years in Tibet." Weird.

"Have you done your homework on the mountain?" he said. Homework? Shit. No, I hadn't. He could tell and was horrified. I could almost hear his disdain simmering.

"Well, it's a mountain that'll fookin kill ya if ya decide to fook around," he said, working his trekking poles. It occurred to me that simply being American might count as fookin around in some people's book. I thought about it. No, I wasn't there to fook around. I was there to do my best, listen to my guides, and have some fun.

Soon after that, the Aconcagua wind blew on us, really blew, for the first time.

Let's talk about the wind on Aconcagua. I want to describe it without sounding like a hyperbolic teenager composing his first tweet, but it's a struggle. I'll say this: I never thought, at 6'1" and 210 pounds, that I'd one day know what it's like to be the sail on a clipper ship. I never thought that I'd have any insight into the life of a tumbleweed, but I do.

I'm not a windologist, but here's what I think: Aconcagua is so tall that the wind has no idea how to handle it. It is, after all, the tallest mountain anywhere outside the Himalayas. The wind blows along, minding its own business, then gets hit by Aconcagua like an elbow right in its face. The wind loses its mind and goes blasting down the valleys instead of staying in the upper atmosphere where it belongs. There are no trees around to impede it, either, so it has a clear shot to harass any Americans who may be fookin around in the vicinity. Presumably, Brad Pitt felt its force same as me during the filming of Seven Years in Tibet, which is just one of the many things we have in common.

That evening we reached Confluencia, a collection of tents and poop shacks in a flat, grassy valley 3400 meters up. I swapped my hiking boots for my Crocs and hiked to the top of a hill near camp with some other members of our six-man party.

Our party consisted of my buddy Mark from Atlanta, who runs an air quality business; Chad, whom we met climbing Kilimanjaro, a biologist and science advocate whom I nicknamed Alpha Dog for reasons I forget; Thor the Danish ultramarathon runner, who lives in Dublin and does collections for an Irish bank; Alan from California, who works in emerging medical technology and loves motorcycles; and the Irishman Darragh, who is a mountain guide and whose gruff, grumpy exterior merely serves as a mask for a deep well of inner gruffness and grump.

On top of the hill we could see up the valley, across a deep gorge cut into the mountain by a river of water running off the glacier. The wind boiled in the dust, whipping up whirling columns. Thanks to these, we could see the gusts coming toward us, and we'd all brace ourselves for them. It was a game: who could lean into the wind the most. We howled and laughed, then came down, ate dinner, and got ready to sleep in the ricketiest wooden bunk beds ever made.

I was slow to stake out my spot in the sleeping tent, so only top bunk spots were left. I wasn't worried about falling off so much as irritating Thor, who was in the bottom bunk. Every one of my movements jiggled him, and every one of his jiggled me, the bed frame itself creaking and protesting all night long. I think he got the worse end of the deal; I'm told I'm a fairly wiggly sleeper. We got through it, though, with the exception of a single pee break for me. I went out in Crocs, underpants, and a down jacket. I would soon come to look back on the idea of a single pee break during a night of sleep with great fondness and longing, or "flongness."

3 DAY TWO

The following morning was Christmas day. We set out for Plaza Francia, colloquially called "mirador," which translates to "place with a decent view," on an acclimatization hike to 4500 meters. Getting accustomed to high altitude is a lot like getting into a hot bath. You go up until you can't take it, then back down, then go up a bit farther, and repeat. In this way you maximize your exposure to high altitude, letting your body know that it needs to get used to it, without actually trying to sleep at altitudes your body isn't used to yet, which it will stubbornly refuse to do.

The trail left Confluencia, heading northwest for the river, which is made up of water melting off the Ventisquero Horcones Inferior glacier. That glacier forms the valley floor at Aconcagua's south face. It's called a "ventisquero" instead of a "glacier" because the Argentines needed a name for it before the French showed up in the Andes with their fancy word "glacier." Nowadays, Spanish has the word "glaciar," but Horcones Inferior is still stuck with "ventisquero."

The valley is hook-shaped, with the outside of the curve resting against the base of the mountain. The south face of Aconcagua looks a bit like the inside of the heap of cocaine into which Tony Montana, played by Al Pacino, was plunging his mug at the end of Scarface. Spoiler alert: do not snort cocaine this way. Actually, it's probably best if you don't snort cocaine at all, now that I think of it. The point is that the south face of the mountain is a nearly sheer cliff that soars 2500 meters or so from the valley floor.

We ate Christmas lunch on the leeward side of a rock as the wind scoured up the valley, all of us looking out over the glacier at the mountain. We were up high enough that we had a good look, unobstructed by the smaller attending mountains crowding around. Our head guide, Seb, attempted to give us some sense of scale. He said "You see that snow field there? That is about 200 meters across." Oohs and ahs were sighed by the climbers. Seb pronounced "meters" as "mitters."

The view was one of those things that a picture just cannot capture. Oh sure, pictures of it are beautiful, but it's not the same as being there. If you fancy yourself a writer, and there's a drop of love in your cynical heart, a view like that could turn you a little more philosophical than is, strictly speaking, wise.

I'd already been motivated to compose a poem two days before, back in Penitentes, the last town before we entered the park. The Shining-ish hotel had a computer at the front desk which is more or less connected to the Internet. I decided to use it to send a last tweet in case I should expire from avalanche or overwhelming ineptitude.

a tall mountain is a pretty woman,
and the clouds are hopeful boys
with no idea how to behave.

This is another answer to that "Why?" question. Looking at views in mountain ranges inspires one to any number of flights of fancy. I need that in my life.

Otherwise, what the hell?

We headed back to Confluencia. The wind blew so hard it shoved me down the trail. I had to jog a bit to keep from being blown off my feet, and the Irishman laughed. And then the trail was gone. We stepped with care in loose dirt and over rocks. Maybe a short cut. Did we come this way?

"No. Well…" said Seb, looking around. Finally, he said, "Rock slide."

Far up the wall, shining clean and white in the midst of the weathered rock, was a patch where perhaps hundreds of tons of rock had detached and come sliding down the hillside, obliterating the trail. Dirt and boulders were everywhere. Scrubby plants were uprooted. There were craters deep enough for a man to lie in where van-sized rocks had pounded into the earth. Some of the boulders had collided with ones already on the ground, smashing each other into big sharp-angled shards and chalk. It would have been unquestionably fatal for us had it happened either time we were on that section of trail that day.

"Yeah," said Darragh, "don't bother running from a slide. You'll only die tired."

That was the last day of the trip that I didn't have mountain sickness. Have I mentioned that mountain sickness sucks? Well, it does.

The Earth's atmosphere is comprised of about 21% oxygen. We humans breathe the atmosphere into our bodies by way of our big dumb faces, and then our bodies select oxygen molecules and exchange them for carbon dioxide molecules. Nitrogen, the most prevalent gas in our atmosphere at around 78%, gets ignored for the most part. Sorry, nitrogen. It's not you, it's us.

Is nitrogen listening still? No? Okay, good, because I lied above about it being us, not it. We humans don't respirate using nitrogen because it's boring. Yeah, I said it: boring. Nitrogen doesn't easily react with other elements, which means it doesn't release energy our cells can use to do work. Oxygen, on the other hand, like Dick Bass, is very enthusiastic. It passes into our blood via the lungs, where it is picked up by red blood cells. Red blood cells are able to do this because they contain a molecule called hemoglobin in their cytoplasm, which is a gross goo inside a cell's membrane. Okay, I don't actually know that it's gross, but I'm making a leap here based on my experience with goo. Once stuck to said hemoglobin in said gross goo, oxygen molecules are carried to the body's cells.

The cells, for their part, are busy doing work, whether they are part of an eyelid, clavicle, or butt cheek. They use nutrients and oxygen in order to make energy for themselves, a process which creates carbon dioxide, or CO2. CO2 and oxygen (O2) molecules are similar in that they like having their own space. So, if the CO2 levels in a cell rise, as they will when the cell is doing work, the CO2 molecules will leave the cell for the relatively CO2-free space of a nearby blood vessel, much as a male partygoer might leave a party which has far too many male partygoers. This process is known as "sausagefestation."

Just kidding, it's called "diffusion." As I say, gases like having their own space, so they will move from an area of high concentration to an area of low concentration. When our CO2 molecule steps out into a nearby blood vessel, it is likely to be swept up by a passing red blood cell, because CO2 sticks to the hemoglobin in those red blood cells, and thus carried away to the lungs where it diffuses again through the lungs to outside air.

At the same time as the CO2 level is rising in the cell, the O2 level is dropping because the cell is using it up. O2 riding along on red blood cells in nearby vessels diffuses into the cell because there's a lower concentration there than in the red blood cell's hemoglobin, and it gets used to do more work.

At high altitude, the percentage of oxygen in our atmosphere remains the same as at sea level, but the atmosphere as a whole is less dense. So the red blood cells don't have as many oxygen molecules per breath to collect, which means the energy-producing cellular business gets transacted at a lower rate. The body can adjust to decreased oxygen levels, but it is grumpy and reluctant. It needs time to adjust to lower levels of O2, and it lets you know that it dislikes this process by generally feeling — and I'm using the clinical medical term here — shitty.

Here is a simple guide for approximating the feeling of mountain sickness in your own home, without all the pesky fitness or international travel: first, either get very drunk on low-quality booze or contrive to come down with the flu. Make sure not to drink any water. If you do, you might alleviate some of your symptoms and we don't want that. Do not, under any circumstances, bathe. In fact, for the full experience, you should cover yourself in fine silt and then perform cardiovascular exercise until you are revolted by your own stink.

That's it! Pretty simple huh? Feel that headache? Feel that general malaise? Now all you have to do is walk a couple of miles uphill with a heavy pack on and you're as good as mountaineering!

It was with these exact symptoms that I found myself in my bed on Christmas night, pondering our possible deaths in the rock slide. I was just about to drift off to sleep when a chorus of voices shouted "Feliz Navidad!" Someone began playing a guitar. Another person tooted heartily on a whistle like a referee who had a fight with his old lady this morning and is determined to be heard this time. The whistle tooter even went on a tour around camp, pausing only to occasionally bark yule greetings in Spanish. I considered murder.

The tooter was one of the Aconcagua staff, and they work very hard. They arrive on the mountain around October, set up the camps, and stay on the mountain until around mid-March. Our guide said the staff usually make enough money in that time that they don't have to work for the rest of the year. Even so, that's a lot of work. The camp facilities aren't permanent, so all the kitchen tents and poop shacks have to be delivered, erected, and dug out. The staff sleep in the same tents and have the same limited access to hot showers that clients do for that whole time. With that in mind, could I really begrudge these people a little Christmas night celebration? The answer: yes. I was tired.

I finally got to sleep with the help of my iPhone and its trove of music by such pop divas as Ke$ha, Taylor Swift, and my favorite, Katy Perry. There is, incidentally, much guffawing and eyebrow waggling about my enjoyment of pop divas. A roommate of mine once discovered me listening to Christina Aguilera while enjoying a scented candle and laughed so hard she nearly passed out.

Let me just state publicly here that I don't understand pop music disdain. Pop music is generally written collaboratively by proven experts in the field. It is recorded at the best studios available using the best musicians and engineers money can hire. Those people use all the latest tools and techniques. If we used the best people, equipment, talent, techniques on a movie, it would be a blockbuster. Yet, for some reason, the same people who stand in line for hours to see The Avengers or The Dark Knight Rises, the two highest-grossing films of 2012 in the U.S. market, look down their noses at pop music. Now, one could argue that this disdain festers because pop music is made for teenagers, but I think I could make a case that The Avengers and The Dark Knight Rises, whose stories originate in the realm of comic books, were targeted at teenagers as well. The Hunger Games, third highest grossing film of 2012, was originally a Young Adult fiction book.

Personally, I don't get into Justin Bieber or One Direction, but I do love me a pop songstress, especially on an expedition into the dusty Andes which are mostly bereft of the soothing tones of a woman's voice. In those cases I find Katy Perry's music very soothing, and I don't care who knows. If you aren't a fan, you're just plain missing out.

4 DAY THREE

The next morning, we headed out of Confluencia for base camp at Plaza de Mulas. It is widely regarded as the hardest day of the Aconcagua normal route, second only to summit day.

Most peaks have what is called a "normal" route. This is the route that is generally accepted as the safest and most efficient route to the top. Once a peak has been summited via this most efficient route, however, mountaineers start thinking about other ways to get to the top, much as a married couple might purchase books or videos to learn new techniques of summiting one another.

The trek to base camp from Confluencia is about eight hours' work, minimum. It's around eight or nine miles in distance, and 1000 meters of elevation gain. The real kick in the balls is that the last hour is by far the hardest. For most of the day you're trekking up what the guides call "Broad Beach," which is a valley floor covered with softball-sized rocks. All of Aconcagua is either loose dirt or loose rock, mind you, both of which are welcome to go fook themselves. You have to be careful where you put your feet, which means you have to always be mindful of the trail, which means you don't get a lot of chances to enjoy whatever scenery you're schlepping through. Any fookin around will net you a turned ankle at best and a rather tiresome tumble down a mountain to your doom at worst.

My journal notes describe Aconcagua's ground as "an annoying chili of rock with a sand base."

Once we hauled our carcasses up Broad Beach, we arrived at a dead end. In the stark sunlight stood a roofless brick structure that had been pulverized by stampeding boulders in a slide, and we rested there. Our head guide, Seb, pointed at a nearby sheer cliff face and indicated that all we had to do was walk up that and we'd be at base camp. He neither smiled to indicate that he was joking nor produced a jet pack. Shit.

Ever wanted to be surprised by how vertical a surface a human being can walk up? Ever wanted to see a mule do it too? In either case I can heartily recommend a trip to Aconcagua. It helped a bit to pressure-breathe, which is basically just breathing harder than your body naturally wants to.

The brain tells the body to breathe when either the CO_2 level gets too high or the O_2 level gets too low. At altitude, though, the process gets a little confused. The body will occasionally even stop breathing for 30 seconds or so during sleep. This is called "sleep apnea." It is especially unnerving to hear your tent-mate stop breathing as you're lying awake staring into space. I heard Mark do it a few times, but resisted the urge to shout or do violence to him to wake him up. We'd been warned by Darragh that sleep apnea might happen and told not to freak out.

On Kilimanjaro, near the summit, I felt like I might pass out a few times. I started forcing myself to breathe harder in hopes of packing more oxygen into myself. It worked fairly well, so I employed the same method on Aconcagua. It feels a bit foolish heaving air in and out like that, especially when the guides and porters are so well acclimatized they seem to take no more than a modest sip of air once every twenty minutes or so. Unbelievably, on Kilimanjaro the porters even smoked cigarettes at the summit. The Aconcagua muleteers smoked too, though they only go as high as base camp.

Speaking of porters, a fairly common question I hear back home is "Did you have a Sherpa?" Allow me to disambiguate. A Sherpa is a person who belongs to an ethnic group from Nepal. A porter is a person who gets paid to carry things. Sherpas are typically found on Everest because they live nearby, high in the Himalayas, and are highly skilled mountaineers. Of course, a Sherpa could conceivably emigrate from Nepal to Argentina and accept employment there as a porter, but I don't think that has ever happened. Most of the Aconcagua porters, from what I could see, appear to be college-aged Argentine kids. They make a living ferrying gear around, but they aren't servants. They are people with an interest in mountaineering who don't yet have the experience or training to be guides. A job as a porter is an entry level position. Our head guide Seb started as a porter something like twenty years ago, and is now among of the most respected men on the mountain.

It was the same on Kilimanjaro. The head guide is the most experienced person on the mountain, and they typically get that way by spending many years there. It's not possible to walk onto a peak and begin making money as a guide unless you know the mountain inside and out. You need to know the weather, plants, animals, best routes, alternate routes, resting spots, where the shade will be at what time of day, everything.

Porters on Kilimanjaro carry most of a client's stuff. As a client there, I woke up in the morning, got out of my tent with a day pack on and started walking. The porters break down the tents, pack up camp, hoist it onto their backs, then pass all the clients on the trail and make it to the next camp fast enough to fully set it up before the clients arrive. It is an amazing feat to see. I carried some of my own crap for a few days on Kilimanjaro and the guides chided me for it. What was I thinking, they asked. That's what porters are for, they said. If clients carry their own gear on Kili — which is, let's face it, the seven summits version of kindergarten — there is less work for porters who make their livelihood there. Also, clients are likely to wear their soft un-acclimatized asses out and not be able to make the summit, which is bad for business. It's better for everyone if the porters do their job (hard work), and clients do theirs (supplying income for porters).

Porters on Aconcagua do less client-crap-schlepping, mostly because Aconcagua has mules to haul stuff as far as base camp. At the high camps, porters help out by carrying tents, water, cooking gas and other equipment upwards in support of the guides, who already have their hands full encouraging a bunch of whiny, headachey clients. Porters will carry all of your gear for you if you want, but it's an extra fee in the hundreds of dollars range. No one in our party took advantage of this, but I'm told some clients do. Our packs did get somewhat heavy at a few points late in the trip, but the physical exertion of the trip really isn't that big a deal. All six of us are reasonably fit people. What is a big deal is the altitude.

I was starting to feel some of the effects of altitude near base camp. When I got tired I would rest a bit. A base camp trek rest stop usually looked something like this:

1. Drop trekking poles.
2. Take pack off.
3. Rummage in pack for camera.
4. Realize if the camera comes out it'll only have to go back in again.
5. Decide not to take a photo after all.
6. Look at pack.
7. Ugh.

On the way up the cliff face, just before we made it to base camp, a mule fell. The muleteer handled the fall by shouting derisively at the animal and throwing a few rocks at it. The mule handled it by thrashing wildly with body and legs. Eventually the thrashing, seemingly by chance, brought the mule's legs into contact with the ground. It stood up and continued down the cliff face seemingly unperturbed. I'm no muleologist, of course, so I'm just going by body language here. Do mules frown? It's hard to tell because their mouths are pointed at the ground. In any case, this one didn't seem harmed by the yelling or the rocks, let alone the fall.

During this walk we also exited the sphere of earthly plant life. The high Andean desert is already free of trees, but above 3600 meters or so even low bushes and grass say "hell with this." Personally, I find the lack of plants to be a bit depressing. Without them, you might as well be standing on the moon, except you don't get to wear a badass suit or blast off in a rocket. Well, I guess that's not entirely true, you do get to wear some fancy outdoor gear, but you have to buy it all yourself and it doesn't come with cool patches. Once atop the wall below base camp, we found ourselves on the face of a strange planet where knife blades of ice taller than a man grow out of the ground. These are called penitentes. Seb was vague about how they form.

The high Andean penitentes were first described by Charles Darwin, who passed through the Aconcagua area on March 22, 1835. His journal, The Voyage of the Beagle, notes:

"...In the valleys there were several broad fields of perpetual snow. These frozen masses, during the process of thawing, had in some parts been converted to pinnacles or columns, which, as they were high and close together, made it difficult for cargo mules to pass. On one of these columns of ice, a frozen horse was sticking as on a pedestal, but with its hind legs straight up in the air."

Darwin thought the horse must have fallen headfirst into a hole and died there, only to become a morbid sculpture when the snow melted away around it. I didn't see any suspended horses on the penitentes, but we definitely saw a large number of mule skeletons scattered about.

Louis Llioutry, a French glaciologist, had a fair bit to say about penitentes in his 1998 page-turner Glaciers of the High Andes, though he called them "penitents." When water vapor molecules are in the air, if the temperature drops, they occasionally condense into liquid water. This is why there's sometimes dew on the ground in the mornings back home, because the ambient temperature has dropped below what's called the dew point. Barometric pressure and humidity of the air also factor in here, but we're ignoring them for simplicity's sake. The dew point in the high, dry Andes, however, is actually below freezing, so when water vapor gets tired of being in the air and decides to condense, it skips the liquid phase altogether and goes directly to ice. This process is called "sublimation," which should be a word that means "rocking out to California ska punk band Sublime," but isn't.

According to Llioutry, this ice then gets melted away in an interference pattern due to the high wind's effects on solar radiation. If you're confused here, don't worry. I am too and I researched the topic extensively. The upshot is that big weird blades of ice form, and they stand shoulder to shoulder in the same direction as the sun travels overhead.

Penitentes remind me a lot of the Joy Divisions' famous "Unknown Pleasures" album cover, which is apropos given that pleasure of any kind is almost unknown at the altitude where they form. Side note: my patient and amazing editor, Karin Beuerlein, whose services you should absolutely seek out if you have some words you need cleaned up, has concerns that the above Joy Division reference is "too arcane," but I trust that anyone interested enough to wonder what I'm talking about will leap joyfully into a Google image search and find pleasure there.

On the outskirts of base camp there were a couple of

small buildings. One had a huge condor painted on the side.

"Sure," I thought. "How often do they see a real condor up here?"

"Look!" someone shouted. "A condor!"

Sure enough, a real live condor was soaring around near camp. Everyone was amazed. "We never see them up here!" they said.

Did you know that the Andean condor voids its bodily waste onto its own legs? This is called "urohydrosis." Some birds do it in order to cool themselves down, but the condor lives at such high altitude that this isn't necessary. As such, we can assume that the condor does this just for fun. Truly majestic bird, the condor. Loves a good leg shitting.

I was among the first to get up the cliff and trudge into camp, which made me feel good about my chances of making the summit. My mountain sickness headache, however, was beating a legendary drum solo deep in my skull. We arrived at the Francisco Hernandez mess tents. These were constructed of metal frames with heavy rubberized skins draped over them in a half cylinder shape. If you imagine a gigantic soup can, perhaps 20 feet in diameter, which has been cut in half lengthwise and then laid on its side, you'll have an idea of their shape.

Aconcagua's base camp, also called Plaza de Mulas, Spanish for "Mulapalooza," is situated in a huge bowl, formed on the east by the towering Aconcagua, which is on the climber's right as he arrives. The bowl is rimmed on the north and west sides by lesser peaks and glaciers. I'm calling these peaks "lesser," but they are taller than anything the American Rockies have to offer. Each guide company has its own bright color scheme for its base camp tents, which are clustered around in a way that suggests that they're organically arranged on the tilting landscape wherever flat spots can be found, or made. Francisco Hernandez tents are white and yellow, for example. Others are orange or red. Many are of the gigantic half soup can design, but some are geodesic domes.

Guide services like Hernandez typically have a lot of groups running at any one time, all at different phases of their trip. When we arrived at base camp we met a group of Englishmen who were preparing to make their summit push. They had their own mess tent just as we had ours, but we all had access to a big dome tent in camp. This tent had a padded, carpeted floor and a few bean bag chairs inside, meant for resting or book reading during down time. I called it The Relaxation Dome.

People who wish to climb Aconcagua can hire all levels of service from guide outfits. We had prepared meals served in a mess tent, but it's also possible to save a bit of money by paying just to have your meals cooked for you, which you then eat off whatever rock happens to be handy and mostly flat. We saw a Russian climbing party doing this. Personally, I was glad for every slight measure of comfort possible, but Seb says Russians are impervious to mountain hardships. In fact, he confided that they are sometimes hard to guide because their faces are always the same no matter how they are feeling. I saw them sitting in the dirt eating soup and shuddered.

Base camp also has such amenities as satellite phones, hot showers, Internet connections, a burger restaurant, and an art gallery. Satellite phones are for calling your loved ones and telling them you aren't dead. I dislike talking on the phone even when I'm at home, so I didn't bother with that. A hot shower might have been nice, but I didn't much see the point. I knew that as soon as I stepped out of the shower I'd just get filthy again. Might as well save the money it'd cost to get in it in the first place. I also did not visit the art gallery, although several other members of our party did. The artist, Miguel Doura, bills it as the highest altitude art gallery in the world, but he isn't just making that up. He holds a Guinness World Record for it, proof of which can be viewed at his web site (aconcaguanow.com).

Upon arrival, we met Pablo, the base camp manager, and collapsed into seats around two plastic tables which ran the length of the mess tent. Pablo congratulated us on making it to base camp as members of our party straggled in. Alan arrived last. Darragh took a look at him and said "You look like shit." If he looked like shit before, he looked a lot worse upon receipt of that comment. Alan is a very friendly, positive person who has Himalayan mountaineering experience. He should have been able to get up to base camp without even breaking a sweat, but that's just how it goes with mountain sickness. You can never tell how truly craptastic it's going to be.

We were urged to drink as much Tang as possible. There is plenty of drinking water on Aconcagua, thanks to melting glaciers or melted snow, but melted water contains none of the trace minerals our bodies need. It's mostly pure water.

"When you go for pee, you lose minerals," Seb said. So we mixed Tang into our water to get sugar and electrolytes into our systems. When I relate this story to my American friends back home, they say, "Wait, they still make Tang?" I can assure you that, contrary to popular belief, yes, and Argentina is overflowing with it.

Also contrary to popular belief, Tang was not developed by NASA. It was invented by a man named William A. Mitchell for General Foods corporation in 1957. He was also responsible for Cool Whip, Jell-O, and Pop Rocks. Sadly, he is no longer with us, but his work lives on. (Read more about him in The Atlantic's 2004 article "Tastemaker with a Sweet Tooth.") Tang got a rocket-powered marketing kick in the pants on February 20, 1962, when it joined John Glenn on the Friendship 7 mission, the first to put an American in orbit around the Earth. Presumably, NASA chose Tang for the same reasons that Seb was urging our climbing party to drink it:

because it contains nutrients and a boatload of calories (in the form of sugar) that our bodies need. Aside from being a carbon-based bipedal human male life form originally born in the month of July in the United States of America who has a great interest in space travel, I am proud to have something in common with John Glenn, even if it's just Tang.

In the United States, we aren't drinking Tang like we used to — but to be fair, we're not going into space like we used to either, much to your humble author's great regret. Tang is now apparently a favorite in Brazil, Argentina, Mexico, and the Middle East. According to an article in Fortune magazine, Tang's makers say drinkers in the developing world like it for its "low price and (ahem) nutrition." That "ahem" is the author's, not mine.

Back home, I questioned a physician friend about the dangers of drinking too much pure water. He confirmed that it is a concern, and even gave it a name: osmolarity. Osmolarity is the concentration of any given solvent in a solution. As I learned in high school chemistry, where I won a hard-fought 72% passing grade, if you are pouring something — say, powdered Tang — into a bottle full of water, the thing you are pouring (Tang) is known as the "precipitate," and the water in the bottle would be known as the "solvent." If you then poured pure water in on top of the Tang, you would be decreasing the osmolarity of the drink, because you are reducing the Tang's strength. Sure, you make the Tang stretch farther, but no one likes weak drinks. No one.

Our body needs minerals to form things like cell walls, teeth, and back hair, as well as to regulate some of the body's natural processes. Salt, for instance, is a very important mineral in the body. In the presence of too much water without salt to help the body handle it, humans can become "hyponatremic," which is a condition in which the salt level in the blood drops too low. If we drink too much pure water, we decrease the osmolarity of our blood, meaning that the sodium and other mineral levels go down as measured against the volume of water, which can lead to all sorts of nasty problems. In fact, it can lead to the undisputed heavyweight of problems: death.

These troubles are faced by people who do rave drugs such as ecstasy, because when on those drugs they tend to dance and party like it's a numerically appropriate year as designated by rock/pop legend Prince. During these wild expressions, the drug doers sweat a lot, dehydrating themselves. They also pee a lot if they've been drinking alcohol because it is a diuretic, which means it makes you pee. Drug doers tend not to notice that they are thirsty, though, as they're steadily drinking alcohol and thus have been known to become severely dehydrated and die. Word got around in the drug doer community that dehydration was a problem, though. As such, drug doers started drinking as much water as they could get their hands on while doing their drugs. Some went too far, though, which led to some of them dying of hyponatremia instead. It's a rough life for drug doers.

On the mountain that first day in base camp, Seb recommended that we drink at least five liters of water per day. I ignored him because I didn't want my pee schedule getting in the way of all the sleep I intended to get. After I'd finally been sung to sleep through the Feliz Navidad whistle-blowing festivities of the previous evening by Katy Perry, supported by Taylor Swift and occasionally Adele, I'd awoken in the night so full of pee that I felt like a water balloon with legs. I was pretty wrecked from the hike in to base camp, so I was looking forward to some deep, recharging sleep.

5 DAY FOUR

· Oh, how we laughed on Kilimanjaro, Mark and I. It is a pretty party cake walk.

Imagine making out, let's say to second base, on a summer night in the back seat of a fine car. Let's say this is happening with some hot person on whom you have a crush. Feel those glorious titties? That's Kilimanjaro. Now imagine being punched in the face, then tied up and dragged down a dirt road behind your worst enemy's shitty pickup truck on a day so hot even your shoes are sweating. That's how I was feeling about Aconcagua.

My plan was to take it a bit easy on the Tang on the evening of day three, against the advice of the guides, so I could sleep through the night uninterrupted by the need to pee. Instead, I awoke in the early morning hours on day four with a pounding headache and deep general malaise. I blundered out of my sleeping bag like a desiccated zombie and headed to the faucet by the mess tent, but it was frozen solid. Shit. Luckily Mark had a couple of liters of water back in the tent, which I downed. Mark asked if I was okay and I moaned at him, then collapsed.

The lesson here is "Do not ignore your guides." They do this all the time. They don't say things to clients

31

because they enjoy the musical sound of their accented English. They say them because they want to help clients. Don't be like me. Listen to them every time. And don't do drugs. You might die from too much or too little water, or possibly even too much drugs.

In the morning, my headache was still with me and so present it should have a name. Chuck the Headache, I thought on the way to the mess tent for breakfast. Or maybe Phil? Yes, Phil the Headache.

Day four was a rest day for us, so when we weren't eating, Mark, Phil the Headache, and I lay in our tent and counted the days until we'd be back down at base camp. Five days. No, six. Possibly more if we were forced to take weather days at the top. The guides build a few extra days into the program. These extra days are there in case the party climbs to the top of the mountain and there's a storm at the top which prevents a summit bid. In that case, we'd wait out the storm near the top. I didn't want there to be any weather days. I wanted to be off the damned mountain as fast as possible.

I was slamming Tang at this point, trying to kill Phil. Tough bastard he was, though, and the byproduct of this murderous initiative was a river of urine.

Now, when we climbed Kilimanjaro, Mark and I had both brought little eight-ounce pee bottles we'd bought at REI. These are recommended purchases because no one wants to get out of their sleeping bag or tent to pee when its freezing-ass cold outside. Only Mark ever used his on Kilimanjaro, at Barafu camp. I think he only tried it then because he felt he'd brought it all that way and he might as well piss in it at least once. I courteously turned away from him as he did his business, but I could hear the liquid filling the bottle up, getting near the top.

"It's down to the wire!" Mark said urgently, but dribbled off just in time.

On Kilimanjaro, though, we never had any real reason to chug water. I never had any symptoms of mountain sickness of any kind until the summit, and it was mild there. On Aconcagua we were asked to drink five liters of water a day, which I was absolutely inclined to do having learned my lesson that first night in base camp. I didn't want to spend another night without any sleep due to mountain sickness. Drinking that volume of water in hopes of combatting mountain sickness, though, makes it almost impossible to sleep longer than a few hours at a time for other reasons. You enter a cycle: Drink a liter of water. Sleep two hours. Wake up. Pee out a liter of water. Repeat. Failure to repeat this process only makes Phil stronger and your sleep more restless. You must also have the mental discipline to unzip your sleeping bag, locate an empty, or mostly empty, pee bottle and pee as soon as you wake up. Lying in the cold and dreading getting up — because it'll be cold and Phil will pound like a sumbitch when you're upright — is only wasting time you could be spending asleep, and you need every minute of sleep you can rip from Phil's slavering maw. I went to bed every night well before dark and didn't move again until breakfast was served, usually at 9:30AM.

Since we'd been warned that we'd be peeing a lot more on Aconcagua than Kilimanjaro, Mark and I had both upgraded to one-liter Nalgene bottles both for pee and regular drinking. We marked the pee-designated bottles emphatically with stickers and permanent markers. Upon seeing our pee bottles so adorned, Darragh remarked, "Meh, drinking out of your pee bottle is no big thing. What's really weird is when you drink out of someone else's." Mark also brought a collapsible 32-ounce bladder, and we both brought our small bottles from the Kilimanjaro trip.

In one night of Tang-fueled urinating on the mountain, Mark and I filled all of these up, emptied them in the middle of the night, and then filled them again. In the morning, not without a measure of pride, we called the guides over to look at our collection of filled pee bottles.

They marveled at them. Passersby also were amazed.

As proud as we were, though, opening the tent to empty pee bottles negates the purpose of the pee bottles, which is to prevent tent opening. We asked Seb if he had any suggestions, and he produced a gallon plastic bottle. It was a big improvement since it meant we didn't have to get out of the tent at night to empty bottles or hunt around for empty ones anymore, but it did mean Mark and I would be peeing into the same plastic jug. I don't mean to brag, but the jug's opening wasn't nearly big enough to accommodate either of our urine delivery apparatuses. Neither of us wanted to spray hot gold all over ourselves, or worse, our sleeping bags, so we were obliged to perform a docking maneuver of sorts. Long story short, he and I have had each other's pee on us. Ah, mountaineering!

Even the big jug proved to be too small on a few nights. We were drinking well over five liters a day at this point. That's how badly I wanted to kill Phil the Headache. Still, he clung to life. Fuck you, Phil. Fuck you so much.

Phil was able to live because my body wasn't doing a very good job of keeping up its oxygen saturation at base camp altitude (4300 meters). The guides monitored our oxygen saturation with a small device called a pulse oximeter. It looked like an overly thick and stubby clothespin. Over breakfast, Seb would say, "I need warm fingers!" and we'd all eat with one hand and stick the other in an armpit to warm it up. He'd then hand the device around the table and check everyone's number by clamping the oximeter loosely on a warmed finger. The device shined a light through our fingers at a detector, then did some science, and finally printed the science out on a numbered display.

Most of the time, normal human oxygen saturation is 99 percent or better. At Confluencia, most of our party were in the mid to high 80s. By the time we reached base camp, some of us had dropped into the 70% range, myself included. That lack of oxygen is why Phil the Headache had set up his drum kit, wedged uncomfortably between the two halves of my brain, and begun pounding away like an animal. What a jerk.

In addition to the breakfast pulse oximetry, our acclimatization progress was monitored by medics stationed at Confluencia and at base camp. If a climber fails to acclimatize in sufficient time, the medics might suggest that the climber take Diamox. They might also suggest that he descend the mountain entirely. I was quite worried that my state would get me sent back down to Mendoza, and while I'd very much have appreciated a few more days of sunny parks and excellent wine, I also wanted to get to the top of Aconcagua.

Diamox, or acetazolamide, its proper name, seems to increase the body's ability to deliver oxygen via the bloodstream, though exactly how it does this is unclear. To quote David E. Leaf and David S. Goldfarb, two of New York University School of Medicine's leading Davids, "The actual mechanisms by which acetazolamide reduces symptoms of AMS, however, remain unclear." It is taken prophylactically, which means climbers must place the pills inside a condom and eat it. Just kidding. "Taken prophylactically" just means it's taken as a precaution before symptoms develop. Mark and I both took Diamox on Kilimanjaro before we even got to altitude. Remember, one of the ways the body knows to breathe is by monitoring the CO2 levels in the blood. The prevailing theory has been that acetazolamide appears to monkey with our kidneys a bit, causing the blood to have increased acidity, which then fools the brain into thinking the blood has more CO2 in it than it does, which makes the brain order the lungs to breathe more often. This explanation, however, is not precise enough for Drs. Leaf and Goldfarb.

I was told by my doctor that acetazolamide increases hemoglobin's affinity for oxygen, though I can find no evidence of this in medical journals. Each hemoglobin molecule is like a car. It has four seats which can be filled by oxygen molecules, but sometimes hemoglobin cars leave the lungs with only one or two seats taken. Increasing hemoglobin's affinity for oxygen would increase likelihood that oxygen would fill up all seats of a hemoglobin car, much as one might increase the likelihood that one's date will hop into a car with one by having a nice car, wearing clean clothes, and possibly even taking a shower before one arrives. In fact, this very affinity was the inspiration for Billy Ocean's 1988 hit, "Get Outta My Dreams, Get into My Car." We know this because the original lyrics of the pre-chorus were:

I'm hemoglobin, with affinity for you,

Hey, Cinderella, stick to me like glue.

I'll be your non-stop lover, get it while you can,

Your nonstop molecule, inside a man.

Okay, I made that up, but in any case, we can certainly agree that singing the original Billy Ocean hit out the open window of a vehicle is likely to net one any number of good-looking passengers.

The upshot is that acetazolamide can be a real help to people with mountain sickness, even if it doesn't increase hemoglobin's affinity for oxygen as my doctor, whom I call Dr. Hairdo for reasons we won't get into here, told me. We know for sure, however, that acetazolamide is a diuretic. As we recall from our drug-doer talk before, this means it makes you pee. That being the case, it's a tricky thing to take if you're in, say, the high Andean desert. You want to decrease the mountain sickness symptoms, but climbers are already hammering fluids into themselves to try to get over the sickness. Throwing a piss-encouraging drug into the mix isn't necessarily a good idea.

Back before we even started the trip, we met with Seb in our hotel. One of the questions we asked was about acetazolamide. Seb said the medics on the mountain would examine us and advise us whether to take it. He also said that if we were taking it we should let him know, which I took to mean that climbers regularly showed up with pocketfuls of the drug and took it regardless of what the medics had to say.

Drugs in mountaineering are currently a controversial topic, much as they are in any sport these days. Mountaineering has a slightly different situation than baseball or cycling, though, because there is no central sanctioning body to take control of monitoring athletes for drug use and using fines or sanctions to punish those who are caught. Most mountaineers are private people who just want to get to the top of whatever mountain they've decided to trot around upon, and they're paying good money to be there, so why shouldn't they increase their chance of a summit bid with acetazolamide, or the even more effective dexamethasone? On the other hand, what's the point of having an adventure sport if anyone with enough money and a pocket full of drugs can ascend to the loftiest peaks it offers?

For my part, I decided I would stay off acetazolamide until advised otherwise by the docs. I generally dislike taking pills anyway. I made that decision, though, sitting in a cafe in Mendoza, overlooking a beautiful public park. A week of getting pounded by Phil, nausea, general malaise and a not-insignificant amount of depression later, however, I was ready to eat an acetazolamide burger with a side of fries.

6 DAY FIVE

After the rest day, we headed up Bonete Peak. It's about 5000 meters tall and visible from base camp, although it's several hours' hike away. Getting anywhere in the base camp region takes a long time because the ground is cut through by streams running off the glaciers. In these grow the penitentes, the big weird blades of ice. On day five we not only observed these, but had to hike through a few sets on the way to the base of Bonete. This is a not-insignificant proposition, but it helped a bit that the high altitude ranger station is on the far side of them from base camp, so the rangers are always walking through them, leaving a suggested trail to follow.

On the way we passed the hotel, Refugio Plaza de Mulas. The story goes that the Argentinian government granted someone permission to build the hotel near base camp, then allowed it to be operated there, offering typical hotel services to travelers for 18 years, according to the hotel's web site. The permit was then revoked, and the hotel is now used only by the park rangers. It looked pretty well chained up when we were there, and the park rangers seemed to only be moving around in their building nearby, but maybe they use it for something. Seems a waste to have a big lodge built right there and Russian climbers eating soup in the dust 500 meters away, but the finer points of government regulation are often mysterious to me.

As we walked by the hotel and ranger station, I noticed a rusty wheelbarrow. I pointed to it and asked Seb if he'd take me to the summit in it. "That is a different price," he said.

On the way up, I fell and tore the knee of my pants. My leg was cut up a bit too, but legs grow back nicely after light damage, mostly for free. Pants, on the other hand, cost money. I haven't had those pants repaired yet, by the way. I'm hoping someone will ask me how I got the hole in the knee. "Oh," I'll say, stroking the beard I don't have, "I took a little spill on an acclimatization hike in the high Andes." Whomever I am talking to will then look impressed, then purchase a dozen copies of this very account for distribution. They will then write the sort of glowing Amazon.com review that independent writers depend upon.

At the summit of Bonete, we looked out across the ridges and valleys extending into Chile. Alpha Dog ate a chocolate bar and attempted to deposit the wrapper back in his pack, but the wind whipped it away instead. The wrapper soared up into the air. It was the most beautiful littering incident I have ever witnessed. Unfortunately, I could not enjoy it fully, first because of Phil hammering away at me, but also because I'd just detected a certain pressure in the lower regions of my innards. Uh oh. 5000 meters up a mountain peak, four hours from a poop shack, and I have to offload solid waste. Not good. A race began: me against my colon.

We all headed down Bonete. Alpha Dog fell face first down the trail and scraped his arm up a bit. He was understandably testy about it, and I sympathized. I fell on Kilimanjaro and immediately got salty with a nearby porter who offered to help me. Falling is embarrassing more than it is painful sometimes.

Most of the descent of Bonete was comprised of scree running. Imagine yourself moving like a snow skier without skis and in loose dirt instead of snow. That's scree running. It's a fast way to get to the bottom of a big pile of loose dirt, and it's pretty fun when you're upright. If you go down and begin to skid down on elbows, ass, or face, things get less enjoyable in a hurry.

A few hours later, the party reached Hotel Refugio again and took a break, but I didn't have time to rest. I was on a mission: an emission mission. A few penitentes and an hour later I arrived back in camp, snatched up the key to my favorite of the three poop shacks owned by our guides (oddly, Number 1), reached into my pack for my toiletries, entered the shack and set up shop.

Before the trip, Mark and I purchased a great deal of food. I bought a dozen bags of organic trail mix, figuring I'd have trouble getting vegetables or fruit into my system. I chose the organic kind in hopes that it wouldn't be dusted with a coat of sugar as most store-bought "food" is nowadays. I wasn't diligent enough, however. The trail mix was sugared. Still, I'd be getting some nuts and dried fruit into my system, and I figured that would be good. The only problem is that the chewed-up nuts were not entirely digested by my system, which meant that they came out with the approximate texture of 40 grit sandpaper. For those of you not conversant in sandpaper grades, that is rough. Imagine passing sand and small bits of gravel and you'll know what kind of fun I was having in Hernandez Poop Shack Number 1 that afternoon. I am a great lover of trail mix, and I have eaten it many times, on the trail and off. I'm willing to chalk it up to problems with that particular brand. If you're heading to Aconcagua, though, I'd recommend leaving the organic trail mix at home unless you want an uncomfortable porthole.

7 DAY SIX

The next day we carried gear to High Camp 1. It was another day of going above 5000 meters for acclimatization purposes, but remarkable because it was the first day we were actually walking on Aconcagua proper. I felt horrible, of course. I kept reminding myself that I was on an enjoyable exotic vacation, but it felt like I was wandering around a huge shitty pile of dirt with a case of the flu. My oxygen saturation had dipped to 75 percent when we went to see the medics. I was feeling by far the worst of anyone of the group. Alan's numbers were worse, but he had been put on Diamox (acetazolamide) days ago and was rebounding well.

We met with the medics for the last time before we headed for the summit. I felt they'd surely prescribe Diamox for me since I felt so awful, but they didn't. I despaired, for the first time, that I wouldn't make the summit. I don't mean to sound arrogant, but I'm pretty good at the mental part of endurance athletics. I've finished all distances of triathlon including a full Ironman race. I've done multiple marathons. I have been on a bike for ten hours, for eleven thousand feet of climbing, for a hundred miles. The races were long, but the training for these was longer, often requiring months of two-a-day workouts. I enjoy working hard and I like being wrung out afterwards; I can go inside my mind for many hours at a time and ignore being uncomfortable. I was not at all used to being in such low spirits when presented with a physical challenge.

I went to Seb. I told him everything I was feeling. I said I respected him and Nico and the medics too, and if they told me not to take Diamox I wouldn't, but that I felt like ass and was worried it would only get worse at higher altitude. He said he understood, but that 75% oxygen saturation was within limits and not to worry. I worried anyway, walking up the switchbacks to High Camp 1.

Now, I have mentioned poop shacks in this account, and I think you can probably imagine what I mean when I do. They're four walls and a roof constructed of plywood with a door and a toilet seat. They're each situated over a pit with a big barrel in it. Each morning of good weather in base camp, a helicopter arrives with the sun. It drops off supplies and hauls full poop containers down the mountain.

No mountain poops stay on the mountain. Folks have realized that with the number of climbers, guides, and staff around, there's a lot of poop, and, thanks to the arid nature of the Andes in general and the cold of high altitude, every poop might as well be a diamond because it is forever. In base camp the poop shacks are handled easily enough, which is to say "by someone else," but in the high camps every poop must be pooped into a bag by the pooper. Porters will carry the bags down the mountain. They prefer that they be securely knotted.

At High Camp 1 there is a majestic view, looking out over the base camp valley. The base camp tents below can be easily picked out against the brown dirt, scattered at the foot of the glacier which descends white from the peaks ringing the valley. Hotel Refugio can also be seen, and the park rangers' station, and Bonete, and the mountains rippling beyond into Chile. All of this, my friends, all of this majesty can be viewed while pooping into a bag. For you see, there are no poop shacks in high camp. No. Instead there is a folding chair base with a toilet seat and a blue plastic bag underneath. Around this is a three-sided wall which comes up to a sitting adult's midsection, thus protecting his or her butt cheeks from the view of the rest of their climbing party.

Do you think you have experienced a cold toilet seat? How interesting! Go put your naked buttocks on the seat at High Camp 1 or 2, or worse yet, bare rock at Camp 3, and you'll forever know the true meaning of the words.

The low wall also allows one's fellow climbers to yell things at you, like "Hey man! Are you taking a shit?" Fun times.

Seb approached me that day on the first climb up to High Camp 1. He said he'd discussed matters with Nico and they thought I should go on and take the Diamox. I don't know if they took pity on me or were just sick of me moping up and down their mountain, but I was elated in either case. I took half a pill at dinner and got the first night of restful sleep I'd had since Mendoza. I felt immeasurably recharged, and Phil the Headache even took his drum solo down a notch.

8 DAY SEVEN

Mark and I lay once again in our tent the next day, our second rest day. Talk in camp was all about about two men who'd died up on the Polish Glacier, which is on the south side of the mountain, the side we'd viewed from Mirador. At the time, one man was dead and the other was still on the mountain somewhere, presumably in the same condition. Apparently the second man had spent the night on the Polish Glacier, a tall order for anyone to endure. The first had managed to summit, then descend the far side of the mountain to High Camp 3. There he'd been told to keep descending because the oxygen in his blood was so low, but he was exhausted, so he decided to nap instead. He died in his sleep. The third member of their party managed to climb back down the way they'd come, and survived.

These men had chosen a far more difficult route to the summit than we were taking. They were also without a guide, and had no radio to talk to potential rescuers. Even so, I couldn't help think about the fact that they'd been headed for the exact same place I was headed for.

I used the base camp Internet to post a message to friends and family.

"Okay, this is it. Acclimatization period over. Tomorrow we head up Aconcagua for the summit. If you're warm and breathing normally over the next four to seven days, think of me."

I missed my family and friends a lot, and I hoped I wouldn't have to tell them I'd failed, or worse, haunt them mercilessly after my death.

Now for a word about our base camp tents. They were a dome-shaped fabric affair supported by crisscrossing bendy metal poles. If it's nighttime and there's someone inside the tent with a flashlight, from outside they resemble some sort of paper lantern from a far eastern country. The manufacturer claims they're 85 inches long, but I am 72 inches long and I can assure you that I was touching nylon on both sides. When lying in my sleeping bag, one's chief occupation on Aconcagua, my feet pushed against one end and my head the other.

Thor and Darragh, I discovered later, slept rotated 90 degrees from the way Mark and I slept in our tent, and apparently had plenty of room. I didn't think to ask Thor about it, who is at least 6'2" if he's an inch, until nearly the end of the trip. Apparently, Mark and I were sleeping the wrong way the whole time.

Still, I am far too big to be a serious mountaineer. My options for double plastic boots were limited because my feet are too big. I had to buy special fittings to make my crampons long enough to go on my boots as well. They're not even freakishly big, my feet. I'm a size 12; hardly unheard of. Still, most mountaineers seem to be more like 5'8" and 140 pounds than 6'1" and 210 pounds. This could explain why the tents are so short.

Many hours were passed lying in the tent staring at the mesh pockets sewn into the top. The sun is very bright at high altitude, since there's precious little atmosphere to slow it down. It's uncomfortable to stand around outside in high sun, even with sunglasses on, because the light is so bright. If the wind isn't blowing, one can stand comfortably in base camp in shorts and a tee shirt while the sun is up. Sunburn is a concern. If the wind blows down off the glacier, though, your nipples will flash freeze so fast as to shoot bullet-like off your chest. These forces combine to make the tent a strange place. If the wind isn't blowing, the tent becomes a greenhouse. It can be quite hot inside, making one want to unzip its many flaps and let a breeze blow through. Too many open flaps and too cold a wind, however, can result in a mountaineer wondering how to explain to the park rangers that he's just shot his climbing partner with his tits.

Dinnertime that night included head guide Seb singing Guns 'n' Roses' "Paradise City" into a fully extended trekking pole as though it were a microphone stand. What he lacked in knowledge of the exact lyrics he made up for in enthusiastically repeating the chorus.

Darragh the Irishman sang and danced along to Manu Chao's "Bongo Bong," played on his cell phone for all to hear.

As far as music on Aconcagua, in general, most of the staff are nuts for Jack Johnson. I heard his music floating out of more than one open tent flap. Seb also was a big fan. I don't have an explanation for this, I am merely reporting the facts as I observed them. Maybe it's the juxtaposition of Jack Johnson's island style with the rugged peaks in which these people make their living. Or maybe they just like his voice. Jack Johnson, if you're reading this, think about visiting Aconcagua. You're a god there.

9 DAY EIGHT

In the morning, we packed gear. Mark discovered that mice had gnawed the strap of his pack, and was dismayed until Seb and Nico fixed it with some impressive mountain sewing. The mice had also gotten into some of my food and my hand warmers, but I didn't need either, as it turned out.

Once we'd arrived at High Camp 1, or Camp Canadá (5050 meters), we lay in the tent. Phil, the demon headache from the very butthole of Hell itself, kept me from napping. It had been a moderate day, perhaps five or six hours climbing. Mark busied himself using a permanent marker to draw a face on our enormous gallon jug pee bottle, complete with beard. The face was drawn around the mouth of the jug such that our pee docking procedure took on a certain fellative quality that I found disturbing. He'd also added the words "El Conquistador."

Mark showed me his handiwork, but had neglected to secure the cap on El Conquistador before doing so. A certain amount of piss dribbled onto my arm and side. Suddenly, I was angry. Phil was angry. Mark thought spilling pee on me was hilarious and that made me angrier. Still, what could I do? It's not like he meant to do it, and anyway it didn't matter that much. I already smelled worse than a mule's ass thanks to not having showered in over a week. I rolled over in a huff and went to sleep.

When I woke up, I found a note on my leg.

"I am sorry I spilled some
Of our co-mingled piss on you.
Please forgive me.
Your pal,
Mark"

Now, it isn't always easy to get along with people, but I am not the kind of person to stay mad after a nice note like that, piss notwithstanding. I folded the note up into my notebook for safe keeping, and photographed it when I got home for posterity's sake.

Seb had been promising cheeseburgers at High Camp 1 for days, and when we'd arrived in camp he was as good as his word. They were delicious. Mark and I each ate two. Darragh and Thor ate four each, as I understand it. Darragh looked like he could easily put away four burgers with his stout body, but Thor was a tall, lanky guy. Even so, Thor could out-eat any of us. "Eat fat, stay slim," he liked to say. Speaking as someone who puts on weight at the mere mention of a cheeseburger in normal situations, I don't recommend anyone follow his advice. It probably doesn't hurt that Thor spends his spare time running marathons all over the world, if not ultra-marathons, which can be as much as 100 miles in length as compared with a normal marathon's 26.2.

Seb and Nico filled our water bottles up for us

using snow. Normally at 5000 meters the ground would more or less be covered in snow. It might be patchy, but certainly not hard to locate. This year it was more or less nonexistent. Nico had to walk quite a ways with a shovel to find a snowfield, and even that was thin on the ground. As such, when he shoveled snow into a bucket to take back to the kitchen tent for melting, he couldn't help but shovel up some dirt and gravel as well. The result was that each Tang bottle had a quarter inch sludge of sand and little rocks in the bottom. Tang had become quite tiresome by this point, but drinking Tang in order to replace minerals while sand and bits of rock crunch in your teeth makes it just that much worse.

10 DAY NINE

The next day's hike to High Camp 2, or Nido de Cóndores (Condor's Nest) at 5570 meters, was only three or four hours long. The camp site featured yet another half poop shack, but behind a rock this time so at least one could transact business without being shouted at from camp.

As one climbs higher and higher, the food gets worse and worse. This is because good food is heavy. Gas for cook stoves is also heavy. Climbers end up eating food that is high in calories, but light in weight. We ate a lot of cookies and Snickers bars, and of course washed it all down with a never-ending river of gritty Tang.

My body didn't know what to do with all that sugar, so it just went ahead and flipped out. My heart rate was all over the place, probably aggravated by the lack of oxygen and lack of sleep. I pressure-breathed a lot of the time to try to calm myself, but it didn't really help.

All I wanted to do was make it to summit day. I

didn't care if I ended up lying in the trail and sobbing for my mama, I just wanted to make it to summit day so the frustration would finally end. I was sick of walking up and down, sick of being shitty at acclimatizing, sick of Snickers and Tang, but mostly sick of going slowly. On Kilimanjaro, they say "Pole pole!" It means slowly, slowly, in Swahili. Mind you, so-called "real" mountaineers look down their noses at Kilimanjaro, because it's easy and very accessible. Pretty much anyone can get to the top without issue. Even so, all mountaineers great and small use "pole pole," as a mantra for not rushing upward.

Myself, I was pole pole going ass-nuts crazy waiting for summit day, and there was bad news. Seb had been studying the weather reports before we left base camp and radioing frequently to check it since we'd headed up. He felt we should take a weather day at High Camp 2, where we'd get better sleep. Sleep at High Camp 3 is almost unheard of. He squatted outside our tent and looked in through the door flap to tell us the news.

Shit, I thought. Shit balls ass fuck ass shit ass balls balls balls ass, I thought as well.

"Okay," I said, nodding. I didn't like it, but I was there to do my best, listen to my guides, and try to have fun, so I just had to suck it up and keep any bitching I felt like doing to myself.

I like having experts around me because I do not know everything. I can't know everything; there's too much of it. I think that a lot of people assume that a guide's job is to get a client to the summit. It isn't. It's to keep clients from dying. If you manage to make it to the summit without giving any indication of keeling over dead, then good on you, traveler. The guides will assist you. Otherwise, no one wants to haul your discarded carcass down to base camp. They have a very hard job, guides. Not only do they have to do twice as much work, or more, than the clients do, they also have to put up with clients. I try to be an easy client to deal with, and rule one of being easy to deal with is "No bitching."

I bitched into my journal and retreated once again into the soothing pink world of pop divas.

11 DAY TEN

Day 10 was our rest/weather day. I woke up surrounded by the usual array of Nalgene bottles full of either frozen Tang or frozen piss. Don't worry, I could tell them apart easily by this point in the trip. They taste completely different.

Once dressed, we munched some cookies, then went for a little stroll around High Camp 2 just for funsies. I was breathing like my teeth were on fire and I was trying to put them out by sheer force of breath. We were presented with some very beautiful views of the valleys on the north side of Aconcagua. I attempted to make a snow angel in a snow field we passed, but the top layer of snow had frozen to a hard crust. Instead of a snow angel, I just made an idiot waving his arms and legs.

In camp after our jaunt, we jettisoned everything in our packs that we weren't absolutely sure we'd need for our summit push. I'd brought way too many underpants. I guess when I was packing for the summit I'd thought I might have a modicum of personal hygiene once I got above 5500 meters. I was wrong. I'd become a zombie, not only in attitude and general walking gait, but also in stench. Fuck it.

The guides tried to interest us in hiring porters to carry our gear to the top, but we declined. Porters are so strong and so well acclimatized that they can do in a few short hours what it had taken our party days to do. For a couple of hundred American dollars, they would get up before dawn the next morning, hike up to Camp 2 in a matter of a couple hours, shoulder whatever burdens were too much for our soft asses, haul them up to Camp 3, deposit them, and then be back down in base camp for dinner. Seeing them go up the trail is amazing.

I made a personal decision to carry my own gear to the top of the mountain. I am a grown man, after all, and I can pull my own weight. I also couldn't afford a porter, but that didn't factor into my decision one bit. No, really. Stop looking at me like that. I'm a man, I tell you. A grown man!

12 DAY ELEVEN

The next day, we hiked up to Camp 3. It wasn't a long day, but I was still exhausted. Our party became very strung out, everyone going at his own pace. Alan lagged far behind. Darragh was slow, but he claimed that it was his method to be slow until summit day. Thor also tended to lag behind, but he spent a lot of time taking photos too. I zombied along slowly in a Tang-fueled fever dream. Mark and Alpha Dog climbed cheerfully, seemingly without any ill effects of altitude.

We were now at almost 6000 meters, higher than the summit of Kilimanjaro. The wind howled around us. Strange rock formations encircled our camp site like reaching fingers. I, naturally, had to take a dump. This time there wasn't even a half poop shack to use. I just had to scramble over some rocks so as to be out of sight and set up my office there. The combination of the howling wind, Phil, and a steady diet of Tang, sand, and Snickers conspired to make this one of the least fun experiences in my life. And to top it all off, without even a half poop shack, I had to hold my plastic bag up to my butt myself. God, I thought, trying not to poop on my jacket or insulated pants, I can't wait to have this much fun on Denali or Rainier.

The night was long at Camp 2. We were not so much asleep as in a prolonged daze. Occasionally I'd skim below the surface of consciousness into what could loosely be considered sleep, but then a particularly harsh wind or especially urgent throb from Phil would bring me back up. I also occasionally woke up to snow falling on my face.

Now, you might be thinking, "But surely the snow would be outside the tent," and normally you'd be right. Humans, however, are basically wet bags of meat, every breath heavily laden with water vapor. At Camp 3, the water vapor that Mark and I exhaled rose to the top of our tent, froze, then drifted back down in tiny flakes when the wind rattled our tent. The frozen flakes collected on our sleeping bags and tickled our faces.

I scrawled the shortest entry of the trip in my journal: "Misery, misery, misery, misery." Mark later reported that I moaned a lot in my "sleep" that night. That's how we zombies roll, bro.

13 SUMMIT DAY

I knew it was soon to be summit day when I heard a pot clank against another pot. That sound meant that Seb and Nico had put away their sleeping bags, converting their tent into a kitchen. It wouldn't be long before Seb yelled good morning to us. I felt apprehensive, but calmed myself by thinking that at least it was summit day. However hard that day got, at least it was the last day.

We waited and the wind blew. The sky outside seemed to lighten a bit, but since we were on the west side of the mountain we wouldn't see full sunlight for many hours yet.

We waited and dozed (maybe) and tent snow tickled our faces. Still, we heard nothing from the guides. Then Seb called good morning to us, doing a not-half-bad Robin Williams from "Good Morning Vietnam," and it was time.

We'd been told to dress inside our tents to preserve warmth, which we did. Nico appeared with a plate of incongruously cheerful cookies for breakfast. Some were flower shaped, with scalloped edges. Some were round with holes in the middle. A machine somewhere had been programmed to draw little designs in chocolate icing on them. They were clearly meant for a grandmother's afternoon or to ride to school inside a plastic baggie in some kid's lunchbox. Mark and I nibbled at them. Neither of us had much of an appetite, even for a pretty plate of cookies. Then it was time to clamber outside, which I did clumsily thanks to huge puffy expedition mitts, heavy double plastic boots, and a stark lack of natural grace.

I brought a great many hand and foot warmers with me in hopes of returning to the States with the same number of fingers and toes I'd left with, which, incidentally, is not 10. It's more like 9.9. I'll explain:

When I was 16, I was helping to build a tent platform on a mountainside. I was with a small group of people, each of whom were carrying a single cinder block up a trail to the site where the tent platform would be. A cinder block is also called a "concrete masonry unit." That's a concrete building block which, here in America at least, is 16 inches by 8 inches by 8 inches. They have two holes in them. Looked at from the hole side, they resemble a giant capital letter H with the ends blocked off.

Where I'm from, in the southeastern United States, cinder blocks are often called upon to fulfill many roles, some for which they were designed, and some not. For instance, if you need to level up your double-wide trailer on a sloping plot of land, you're probably going to use cinder blocks. That's more or less a proper use of them. Then, however, if you need to construct a set of stairs up to the door of said double-wide trailer and you can't afford the wood to construct those stairs, you can just stack cinder blocks in a stair shape. The folks who build double-wide cinder block stairs often forego such trifles as mortar to hold them together, so if you should encounter a set of them, take care. In fact, if you should have occasion to walk up a set of these stairs, it's probably best if you take a few moments to take a hard look at the direction your life is heading. Are you about to purchase methamphetamines? Don't do that. Are you about to enter someone's hunting lodge? That might be okay. I digress, but seriously, don't do meth.

Long story short, if you've ever spent any time staring at a public school or jail cell wall, you were likely staring at a cinder block. I have stared at both.

I was carrying one of those on my back up a muddy trail and my right foot slipped. I put my right hand down on a rock to steady myself and the cinder block fell on said hand resting on said rock. The sharp edge of the cinder block striking the rock with my hand in between caused my right ring finger to become mostly divorced from the rest of my hand, which was especially troublesome given that I was out in the woods, the better part of an hour separating my location from the nearest hospital. Some spirited driving followed, then some surgery and some recovery, and I'm happy to report that my hand works fine. I can type or play the piano just fine, or at least as well as I would do those things if I had ten complete digits. You'd have to look closely to know I have one reassembled finger, and typical daily social interactions do not require those around me to examine my hands. I call it my Frankenfinger.

Even though I only have the 9.9 fingers, I still wanted them to be warm and I wanted them to come home with me not at all frozen off, which is why I bought the hand and foot warmers. The only problem is that hand and foot warmers get warm through a chemical reaction that requires oxygen. If you have cold hands or feet at sea level, they work a treat. At altitude they might as well be little baggies of day-old condor squeeze.

Outside the tent it was cold. I thought I knew what cold was until I got outside that tent and entered a graduate level course on the subject. It was cold in exactly the same way that money is "useful" or that Joseph Stalin was "a dick." There was light enough to see, but it was dim and diffuse.

The guides had filled our Nalgenes with boiling water so they wouldn't freeze as quickly. I began collecting my bottles from the pile on the ground and shoving them into my pack, but I was stopped. I was told I had to put Tang in them. Sigh, Tang. I looked at my big puffy expedition mitts. I looked at the small fiddley paper packets of Tang. Shitcakes. I was gonna have to take off my mitts in this crazy cold.

The next few minutes just sucked. I was ripping open packets of Tang to pour the powder into my Nalgenes with the damned wind blowing and my dumb fingers feeling like they were gonna snap off at any moment. I had on thin wool gloves, but they were nearly useless in that cold. Finally I Tanged my bottles and stowed them away and was ready to walk. My hands hurt like crazy. My thumbs were totally numb. Seb told us to move our fingers at all times to keep the blood flowing, which I did. My thumbs would be tingling for days.

Seb said we'd waited until later in the day than usual because he was hoping the wind would die down. He said sometimes he can tell before his party even leaves Camp 3 that no one will make the summit. A huge part of a guide's job is to look at clients and decide whether they are fit enough to continue. They often ask you how you are doing as well, but I have been told that when they do this they've already made a judgment about your fitness.

They just want to hear what *you* think about your fitness. When the wind is really bad, Seb takes the party uphill anyway, until they can't take the wind and the cold and turn back. No one wants to hear that they can't make it. They want to at least try. He didn't say for sure whether our day was one of those days.

A huge part of completing any long physical task is mental game. It sounds flippant when you're hobbling along late in a marathon and someone runs by shouting "This is 90% mental!" but it's true. First you have to have the self-confidence to force yourself to sign up for whatever it is. According to Running USA's yearly report for 2013 (runningusa.org), nearly four times as many people finished a half marathon (1.85 million) as full marathons (487,000) in the United States in 2012. I think the difference is down to people thinking a full marathon is astronomically harder than a half. It's not, really. I'm not a runologist, but I think if you can do a half, you can, and should, do a full marathon at least once. You don't have to be fast. Just suffer through it. Later on, details like how long it took you are easily forgotten, but the fact that you finished will be remembered forever. That said, if you've done a half marathon and you tell people it was a full marathon, or by omission of the word "half" allow anyone to believe it was a full marathon, you are living a life of lies.

The second part of mental game is when it's race day or summit day and everything sucks but you have to keep going anyway. Being slow is fine. Being annoyed is fine. Being last is totally fine. Quitting is not fine. The standard to which I try to hold myself is this: Unless I am unconscious, bleeding profusely (more than a trickle), have broken a large bone, am in grave danger, or an official tells me to stop, I have to keep going. So far, I have been able to abide by these rules. There may come a day when I quit just because I'm lazy, but I hope not. I would feel pretty bad about myself.

We walked uphill in the mostly dark. Excuse me if I am skipping hours of toil here. There isn't that much to say about walking up a dusty trail while flexing and extending one's fingers and wheezing like a mattress in a honeymoon suite.

Eventually we reached the first of four landmarks along the trail, White Rocks. The guides gave us some hot tea, and we saw the sun for the first time. Seb disappeared for a few minutes, then came back.

"I try to take a shit and froze my ass," he said.

I will skip more boring hours of walking and wheezing here as well. That done, we heaved ourselves up a steep 50 meters or so of trail to a flat area with a small wood structure called Independencia Hut. Even by hut standards, it was a shithole; the roof and some of the walls were missing. I was grumpy, but the good news was we were halfway done with summit day.

Two bits of bad news: the wind was killer, and there was no snow on the canaleta. Snow is good because the guides kick holes in it as they go up, and then all you have to do is stick a boot in the already-made hole and step up. Easy. Since there was none, we'd be slipping and sliding in an upwards direction (we hoped) on the same loose rock we'd been on all week, the wind pounding and leaching heat out of us the whole way

There was much discussion between Seb and Nico about whether we'd press on at all because of the wind. A group ahead of us was huddling in the middle of the next section, called the traverse. "Traverse" means simply to "go across." In mountaineering terms, it means traveling parallel to the ground rather than up or down the mountain's slope. Rarely is the easiest path up a mountain a straight line from bottom to top. The group ahead was huddling at a small rock outcropping called the Finger, waiting for the wind to die down. We had another four to six hours ahead of us, and the guides asked us to be honest with ourselves and them.

This was it.

"If you don't think you can make it, turn around now. We only have two guides and I can't send you down by yourself. If you are thinking of quitting, now is the time," Seb said.

I checked myself over. I was conscious. I did not appear to be squirting blood. My bones, large and small, were intact. I was in no particular danger, and no one was telling me I had to stop. So, I had to go on. I looked at Mark. He did not appear to be unconscious or squirting blood either. He even gave me a nod. Good to go.

Alan, though, raised his hand. He'd been battling mountain sickness since we first hit base camp, and he'd had enough. Luckily, a passing guide from another group happened by, so Seb and Nico were able to send Alan down with him. They both stayed with our remaining five members. Keep in mind here that Alan is a healthy, strong, positive person with plenty of mountaineering experience. There's no reason he shouldn't have been able to continue except that that's just how mountain sickness is. You never know who it will hit, how hard, or when. Every step upward is a roll of the dice.

That handled, the guides prepped us for the traverse. We'd be walking directly into the wind. Any exposed skin would be frostbitten, so we were told to walk at an angle so that our parka hoods would partially shield our faces. I borrowed Nico's pocket knife to cut a breathing hole in my buff, which is a stretchy piece of cloth I wore around my neck.

The wind on the traverse was obscene. It blew without even a hint of slacking, like an ice-cold blowtorch. I realize that is a crap simile because blowtorches are not at all cold. I also considered "ice cold jet engine" but jet engines are not cold either. In fact, in pretty much any instance, molecules of air moving quickly equals heat. That's what temperature is: a measure of how fast molecules are moving. The faster they move, the hotter they are, except near the summit of Aconcagua, where they are quite fast, quite cold, and difficult to compose similes about.

I didn't enjoy the experience of being on the traverse, although it was kind of neat to look all the way down the mountain to base camp. The little tents were just discernible: tiny yellow or red or white pixels against brown dirt. The view ahead, on the other hand, was less majestic.

At the far side of the traverse, the trail just goes straight up in the air. It looks like a graph of a quickly rising stock's share value. The guides had warned us that this part of the day would be so slow that we'd be within conversation distance of people who were an hour ahead of us on the trail. This was not a lie. That's how slowly we were moving.

I was very lucky. I was able to stay right on Nico's heels, arriving first of our party at the cave at the base of the canaleta.

Next to arrive were Thor and Darragh. We sat and drank hot tea from Nico's thermos.

The canaleta is a roundish half-pipe gully between two jutting ridges that run down the mountainside, wider than what they call a "chimney" and not steep enough to be what they call a "couloir." It is the last section before the summit, and the base of the canaleta is where the guides decide who in their party is strong enough to continue and who will be turning back to Camp 3.

"If you want to reach the top from here," Nico said. "You will drink one liter water." I downed a liter of water.

Alpha Dog arrived next with Seb, and flopped on the ground. I thought he was just tired, but he was in a huff as well. Seb said they'd be turning around. Seb judged Alpha Dog too slow to make the summit and get back to Camp 3 before sundown.

My buddy Mark was also unlucky. He'd gotten so low on oxygen that he "felt drunk." He and I have been wildly drunk together enough times that I know he knows what he means. He was unable to place his feet or trekking poles properly on the trail. Seb spotted his difficulty and told him his day was over.

Unfortunately, Mark had the point-and-shoot camera I'd intended to borrow to take a photo of us should we both make the summit, and he was told to wait down the trail from where I was. I left my camera in base camp because I got sick of carrying it around.

Seb and Alpha Dog and Mark headed back down, and Nico, Thor, Darragh and I all prepared for the final push. The summit would be two hours or so from where we stood. We dropped our packs, munched a Snickers, tucked a Nalgene into our parkas inside pockets so our body heat would keep them from freezing, and set off. My luck held and I was able to stay with Nico up the canaleta. He coached me on my breathing, which was even harder and more urgent now. He urged me to slow my breathing and step in time with my breaths, which I did. He was right. Listen to your guides, folks. Listen. To. Your. Guidesssssssss. Do it.

The whole way up the canaleta we could see people peeking over the edge of the summit. Those bastards! How I hated them. All right, all right. Sorry, guys who summited before we did. I got a little huffy back there, what with the altitude and all. I'm sure you're not bastards.

Other points of interest along the canaleta included views in every direction of deep blue sky, and a pile of vomit hoarfed up by some climber earlier in the day.

After much breathing and slow-stepping, I arrived, still on Nico's heels, at the last two steps to the summit.

"Hand me your camera and I will video you walking up," he said, but Mark had the camera in his pocket somewhere on the way back to Camp 3. You'll just have to imagine, if you can, what it might look like when a tired guy in a parka walks up some rocks. Thor and Darragh soon arrived, and we took a few pictures with their cameras.

Aconcagua's summit is a mostly flat expanse the size of a medium nightclub dance floor. It tilts a bit, but a reasonably talented bike rider could ride around in a circle without running off the edge. He'd have to bring the bike up first, though, which, according to Seb, someone has done. The sky is enormous, and smaller peaks stretch away below. Even the clouds seem to be below you. If you've flown over a mountain range in an airplane and looked out the window you can probably imagine what it looks like, but it is a very different feeling standing there with all of the mountain under your feet.

I suppose I should have felt elated and accomplished standing up there, but I just felt tired and ready to get back down safely. Darragh turned to me and said, "You know, for a fookin American, I'm impressed. Fair play."

Because of the way our Earth is tilted away from the sun, the Southern hemisphere, where Aconcagua is, has its summertime at the opposite point in the year from the Himalayas. The Himalayan range is where the tallest and most dangerous mountains in the world, including Everest and K2, are. In December and January, everyone in the Himalayas retreats below 5000 meters or so because it gets so frigid and so snowy any higher up than that. Because of this, it is entirely possible that Nico, Thor, Darragh and I were the highest-altitude people in the world at the moment we were on top of Aconcagua. We stood at 6962 meters, or 22,841 feet if you prefer a bit of fookin around.

14 DESCENDING

Mountaineers will tell you that getting back down from a summit is often the most dangerous part of the whole trip. Actually, it's medical researchers who say that, but mountaineers repeat it, and in my experience it is true. Perhaps it's because it's easier to really dig your toes into the ground when you're going up. I'm not a footologist, mind you.

I fell more times than I can count descending from the summit of Aconcagua. Once, I went down in some boulders near the base of the canaleta with my leg twisted painfully underneath me. I thought for sure it would be completely smashed up when I got off it, but nothing was broken. For all the times I fell, I sustained no serious injury, nor did anyone in our party. We were very lucky.

I was ahead of everyone descending the canaleta to the cave, so I sat on a rock for a bit to wait. I fell asleep, had a brief dream, then woke up when my body sagged enough that I was in danger of slumping off the rock. This entire sequence took perhaps two or three seconds, but it was weird and it spooked me a bit. I decided not to doze off like that again.

Once we'd shouldered our packs once more at the base of the canaleta, we all set off for Camp 3. Heading back the way we'd come, Nico and Thor took off. I wasn't even back to the Finger yet when they disappeared over the hip of rock that obscured the Independencia hut from my view on the traverse. I felt like I'd already expended a significant amount of effort for one day and wasn't in any hurry, a sentiment apparently shared by Darragh who was even farther back. Also, I was busy falling on my ass every few minutes. Each time I fell, I looked around to see if anyone had seen it. Thankfully, I was alone, and my climbing party were quite used to seeing me flopping around on the ground by this stage of the game.

The climb to the summit from High Camp 3 took around nine hours, but going back the other direction consumed less than four hours. It's a strange feeling, that speed difference, like watching one of your hardest days over again on fast rewind. I stalked with ease past rocks I had sat gasping for breath on only hours before.

The incongruously pretty plate of cookies had reappeared on the ground when I returned to Camp 3. Thor was lying in the dirt next to it, munching on them. I flopped next to him and munched a few myself, then crawled into my tent to find a fully clothed Mark lying on his back. He didn't move or otherwise acknowledge that a person was crawling in, so for a moment I was worried. Then he spoke.

"How was it?" he asked.

"Horrible," I said. "Worst day of my life. The top is shitty."

"Good. I'm glad I didn't go any farther."

The top isn't really shitty. It's breathtaking. I just figured Mark wouldn't want to hear me talk about how much he'd missed out on.

In the morning we packed up camp, then descended from Camp 3 straight through High Camps 2 and 1 to base camp. This took about half a day. When I walked into base camp, Pablo and some other members of the staff were out to welcome us. I took my hat off to mop my sweaty forehead with a shirt sleeve, and got a bit of dust in my eyes, then stood there blinking and tearing up as the staff congratulated me.

"Well, don't cry about it," said Pablo.

Nico predicted that we'd be very glad to see a chair again when we returned to base camp from the summit, and he was right. Chairs are a great invention that I take for granted in my everyday life. A few short days of sitting on misshapen rocks that put uncomfortable pressure on my ass bones made me realize what a luxury sitting can be. Hell, most of the time there's not a suitable rock to sit on at all. Most of the time you're either standing, sitting on the ground, or lying in your tent. The great thing about a chair is your body is fully at rest, but you don't have to expend much effort to convert yourself to a standing position. If you are sitting in the dirt and you have to get up, it can be a tiring process, particularly if you are the host organism for a pounding headache like that old son of a bitch Phil.

Mind you, the first chairs we saw were the cheapo plastic lawn furniture variety that is the standard in base camp. If you walked into a gigantic suburban retail store found in nearly any American community and said "Point me to your very shittiest sitting devices, please," these would be the ones. Even so, sitting in one was magical.

We all ate real food again, which was glorious. The

torrent of Tang and tsunami of Snickers in high camps had left my mouth feeling the way a crappy fluorescent bulb makes things look. The guides asked us if we wouldn't mind sleeping as a group in the Relaxation Dome, as that would save them the trouble of setting up all our tents. We agreed, and all six of us rolled out our beds there. Thor fired up his tablet computer and together we watched Eddie Murphy and Arsenio Hall in *Coming To America*. I have limited experience with slumber parties, but this one was quite nice.

There was a lot of talk about getting lifted back to the park entrance in the helicopter. The stated fare for such a ride was $1500, but it could be split up over three people at $500 each. When word came that it was a cash-only affair, Mark and I figured the walk out wouldn't be so bad in any case.

We hauled all the way back down from base camp, over Broad Beach, across the Horcones River, through Confluencia, over the Brad Pitt bridge and to the park's entrance, a distance of about 13 miles. Along the way we passed many clean and bright-eyed climbers heading into the park on their first day. I privately judged their summit potential as they passed. This one is a maybe. That lady looks pretty fit. This guy, though, has no chance in hell.

Once at the entrance, a van picked us up and cold Coca-colas were distributed to us. Coke is headquartered in Atlanta where Mark and I are from. In fact, some people say if you order a Pepsi in Atlanta your name goes into a secret file and you get special critical attention from parking attendants and police. I don't know if that's true, but it was a nice slice of home.

Back at the Shining-esque hotel in Penitentes, we changed our clothes and moved our gear around. There was a very clean family there who were preparing to head up the mountain the following day. They marveled at our dusty, filthy appearances with obvious trepidation. I hammed it up a bit for their benefit by easing my tired bones into a chair and loudly praising the act of sitting. Thor and Darragh weighed themselves and compared their numbers to their pre-climb weights. Darragh won the challenge by losing eight kilograms over the course of the trip.

No one wanted to linger. We all wanted to get back to Mendoza and hot showers, then go out for some dinner, so we piled into the van and set off. The gentleman at the wheel, Gustavo I believe his name was, drove like he was mad at tires and wanted them to suffer. Such was our proximity to death on that drive down the mountain that I head Darragh murmur "I'm not afraid of dying on a mountain, but I don't want it to be in a fookin van."

We were stopped by a military checkpoint. Perhaps they were just police, but they were definitely wearing green army fatigues. They asked us who we were, and where we were going. Gustavo did all the talking. We were on our way again soon enough. I've been stopped like that a few times in foreign countries. Each time it happens, it makes me appreciate my freedom to go wherever I want with whomever I please back home.

Back at the hotel, we all showered. Talk about something a person can take for granted! A hot shower is an amazing thing, even with the dodgy Argentine water temps. We then went out to eat, taking advantage of the usual late dinner time, not to mention the availability of Malbecs, and returned to the hotel for a solid night of sleep.

Phil, that tough old bastard, slipped away overnight. I thought I felt a twinge of his old pounding when I woke up, but I think it was just a remnant of the wine. Good riddance, Phil. Go bother someone else.

We enjoyed kicking around Mendoza once again, then went out to dinner that night with our guides as a big group. Everyone looked peculiar to me because they were clean and smiling.

As we drank, I reflected on the trip. The climb cured me of any desire I had to ascend beyond 7000 meters. While I might someday trek to Everest base camp or around the Annapurna region in the Himalayas just to experience the area and culture, I have no desire to attempt to summit the 8000-meter Himalayan peaks. First of all, in Everest's case, I can't afford it. An expedition there would cost well over what I make in a year. For the cost of a trip to the summit of Everest, you could attempt Kilimanjaro once a year for twelve years, and that's if you tack on a few days of safari and buy new gear each year. Or you could attempt Aconcagua once a year for six or seven years.

I think there is vastly greater benefit in going on trips that are challenging, but not necessarily death-defying. Too many times, I think, we crave extremes when much of the middle is just as amazing, lots less expensive, and much less a pain in the ass.

I want you to imagine an XY chart. It might help to draw a large L-shaped line on a piece of paper. The Y axis — that's the one going up — will be "Danger." The X axis, going left to right, will be

"Difficulty." At the top right of this graph, we might plot an activity that's equally very difficult and very dangerous. That might be summiting Everest or Antarctica's Vinson Massif. At the top left we'd plot an activity that's very dangerous but also very easy. Here I would place skydiving. All you have to do is fall out of a plane. What could be easier than that? Still, it's plenty dangerous. At the bottom, near the crook of the L or the origin of our graph would be sitting on a couch. It's easy and quite safe, which is why most people do it so much. (Side note: sitting on the couch has hidden dangers!) Bottom right we might plot an extremely strenuous workout, since it would be difficult to complete but more or less safe if we're taking proper precautions like not dropping heavy weights on ourselves.

Somewhere in the middle of this graph is the butter zone, where we'd plot activities that are hard but not too hard. Anything that is exciting will most likely, by its very nature, be dangerous, but it doesn't have to be lethal. Everyone has their own butter zone placement, and you should certainly experiment to find where yours lies. I'd plot Aconcagua to the rightward side of my butter zone, but that's just me. As I said at the beginning of this account, I'm not a mountaineer. I'm a guy who likes going outside and then writing jokes about it.

In all seriousness, although Aconcagua was an arduous trip, I am glad I went. I am very glad that I didn't get injured. The sights I saw there with my eyeballs were breathtaking. Most of all, I am glad I summited, because it means I don't have to go back.

THE END

Yes. All right. This is the end of the narrative. There's more writing, but that bit just before was the end. Some beta readers felt that it wasn't clear that the next part is a hilarious appendix, not a hilarious continuation of the narrative which doesn't have, at its end, a definitive end. The end is here. This is it. The Appendix doesn't need an end. It's an appendix. So, the end is this and we are at it.

…but there is a bit more.

.

15 APPENDIX

I mentioned different pieces of gear in the text, but when Mark and I were researching the trip we found a lot of conflicting information about that, so I thought someone might find the following more concise breakdown of what we bought and why helpful. This is not a complete list of everything you need. You should get one of those from your guides.

On a normal backpacking trip, where I have a single pack that carries all my crap for the entirety of the time, I like to pack in "groups." Shelter group, sleeping group, kitchen group, toiletries group, et cetera. Each group goes into its own container, then into my pack in an orderly way so my pack is nice and tight with the load distributed evenly. Then, after the first night, it all goes to hell. Still, I continue to think of gear in terms of groups.

In this case, the shelter group was handled entirely by the guides and porters, so I didn't have to worry about it at all. So, I got that going for me. Which is nice.

Duffel Bags

First of all, Mark and I both used two enormous duffel bags to hold our gear. Outdoor retailers offer duffel bags in various sizes, including the "XXXL" size, which is a whopping 18 x 42 inches with 172 liters of capacity. For you traveling murderers out there, it is easy enough to fit a body inside, unless you fancy murdering typical Americans. These retailers want over $50 each for these, but you can also find similar sized cheapo duffels on Internet retail sites for less than half this price. The name-brand bag is better quality canvas and comes with a small toiletries pouch, but I would caution that these bags are more or less disposable, so the extra expense on the nicer bag isn't necessarily worth it. I had one nice bag and one cheapo bag. Both now have holes in them due to being dragged, tossed, lost, found, chewed through by mice, and lashed to mules. I might be able to use them again on another expedition, but at $20 I might also just buy new cheapo ones.

Once you have your bags, take a big permanent marker and write your name as it appears on your passport, your flight numbers, your phone number, your email address, and any other pertinent information you can think of. Write this information as big as you can on both bags. Then, once your bags are packed, take a color photo of them and make sure you have the photo with you when you are traveling.

Your bags will be lost. Not "might" be lost. Not "perhaps will unfortunately get lost." They will be lost. Be prepared for it mentally and emotionally. The only reason Mark and I arrived in Mendoza with our bags is that we spent most of our layover in Santiago, Chile, standing in line and asking about them. We stood in line until it was our turn, asked about our bags, were told they had no information, then got right back in line at the back and repeated the process. Had I not had a color photo on my phone of my two bags, they would certainly have been lost. On the way home, I didn't care if I ever saw my gear again, so I didn't bother hounding the poor Chileans about them. One got lost. My airline eventually found it a few weeks later and delivered it to me after many phone calls. Bags are lost so often in Santiago that guides build in an extra day before the trip leaves Mendoza to sort this out. I think the baggage handlers in Santiago pull bags off an incoming plane and then just pile them up somewhere, only going through this pile later for bags that someone is asking about. Amazingly, most bags do get found before the trips leave, according to our guides.

Sleeping Group

Past experience with the outdoors, as well as the indoors now that I think of it, has learnt me that I like to sleep well at night. I didn't have a chance in hell of it on Aconcagua, but at least it wasn't because of my gear.

Mark and I had trouble getting an accurate read on what the nighttime conditions would be like. Some accounts we read made it sound like we'd need seventeen sleeping bags nestled inside one another like Russian dolls. Others made it sound like we would be plenty warm in our summer bags from back home. Our official gear list from our guides said we needed a four-season sleeping bag, though, so both of us elected to be warm rather than sorry.

A four-season sleeping bag means the bag's insulation is thick enough that it can be used in the winter. Sleeping bags only meant for use when it's hot outside are one- or two-season bags. It's a confusing system of rating a sleeping bag's warmth, especially when you consider that most mountaineering takes place when it's summertime but still balls cold outside due to high altitude. Manufacturers also rate bags by degrees, though, which is nice, and they even rate them for Fahrenheit degrees for us daft fookin Americans.

I bought an ultralight down bag a while back for use in the mountains near where I live. My friend Mitch Davis at a local Atlanta store called The Gear Revival (www.thegearrevival.com) recommended the manufacturer. I was very impressed with that bag, so I bought another one for Aconcagua from the same company. My bag is rated for −10°F/-23°C and it kept me plenty warm. Mark bought a similar bag from a different company and liked his as well.

I brought two sleeping pads – again, because I wanted to be comfortable. Cold ground has an amazing ability to suck heat right out of your body, and rocks have an amazing ability to poke you uncomfortably in the ribs, hip bone, or ass, so more pads is more better, especially when you aren't carrying them very far. I wouldn't bring two pads on an Appalachian Trail hike, but I know the campgrounds on the AT see a lot more use and have a lot more soft sleeping areas than a mountain has. I brought one typical blow-up style pad and one blue closed-cell foam pad of the cheap kind found at famous big-box retailers.

Outerwear

I knew from past experience that wind can really blow. I also knew that it seriously blows on Aconcagua. When it does, it can remove a lot of things from a person's body, like calories of body heat and units of happiness. Yes, that's right. The wind blows happiness right off you. Look it up; that's science.

As such, I did not skimp on outerwear, which came in three primary forms: soft shell, wind shell, and belay jacket.

I chose a relatively thin soft shell for two reasons. First, I am a walking furnace. I am hot at almost all times. I often sweat a bit during cold showers. At bedtime, I like the ambient temperature in my apartment to be set just below that of your average meat storage facility so I can sleep through the night without sweating too much. Second, it was on sale at half price.

I put on my soft shell on the first night at Confluencia and was swaddled in it more or less for the remainder of the trip. In fact, after I got home and my bags were returned to me, I washed that soft shell and then wore it one cold day in the city and it felt like coming home.

I also did not skimp on my wind jacket. Months before we left I pulled out my previous trusty wind jacket and gave it a critical look only to discover that years of hard use had rendered it shitty. I was willing to overlook a certain measure of shittiness for outdoor cavorting around home, but not on an expedition to Aconcagua. I got a new wind jacket long enough to cover my 6'1" body to a level below where the hip belt of my pack would fall. It also has vertical zip pockets situated high on the body so that they can be operated with pack straps on. These pockets aren't great for sticking hands into, but they are very good for stowing gloves, Snickers, and packets of Tang.

My old belay jacket also got upgraded. When I say "belay" jacket, I'm talking about a puffy down coat that you put on over your soft shell and wind shell when it is very cold and you aren't moving around too much, such as when you're operating ropes in a belay situation. We didn't use ropes on this trip, but I still call this type of jacket a belay jacket. I often wore it at meal times. As stated above, when I am moving around I am very warm. I wore my soft shell for the most part as high as 5000 meters, and only added my wind shell close to 6000 meters. I added my belay jacket over top of the other two for the trek up to 7000 meters.

My old belay jacket didn't have a hood and I knew I wanted a hood for Aconcagua. Hoods on puffy jackets aren't very cool- looking. I wouldn't buy a hooded jacket for wearing on ski trips, but at high altitude, having a layer of down around your melon is really nice. When I ordered it, the guy at my local store said "Oh good, finally someone is ordering a jacket with a hood. Don't know why no one ever does. I love 'em."

Keepin' it hood, y'all.

On my legs I wore trekking pants until 5000 meters or so, above which I switched to hard shell pants. The harder pants are windproof, have strengthened areas on them to make them abrasion resistant, and are able to unzip down the sides to vent heat generated by legs and ass.

Footwear

I brought three layers of footwear to Aconcagua: double plastic mountaineering boots, trekking shoes, and Crocs.

Double plastic mountaineering boots are meant for the summit push, and are actually a boot within a boot. They are extremely warm, as you might imagine. They have huge rubber soles that are good for easily attaching crampons to. We didn't have any snow or ice to speak of on our trip, so we never got to use crampons. We carried them most of the way up the mountain anyway though.

Trekking shoes are single-layer leather or synthetic boots of the kind that anyone would probably call a hiking boot. They provide a decent amount of ankle support and protect your toes from getting stubbed on rocks, which they certainly will on Aconcagua. They're nice because they're a lot lighter than the double plastics, but they're not as warm.

Back home in the Southeast, I typically won't wear hiking boots for multi-day trips. I just wear trail running shoes. Though trail runners typically don't provide any ankle support, they are lighter than hiking boots, which is nice if you're going to be walking a long way. The nicest thing about them, though, is that they dry quickly. My home region is a pretty wet place with a great many stream crossings. Hiking boots are typically lined with a breathable waterproof material, but if you should have to cross a stream whose water is deeper than the top of the boot, no amount of waterproofing is going to save your feet from being wet. Wet feet aren't a problem, but wet feet that don't soon get dry are. Aconcagua, though, is very dry and very rocky. Trekking boots were a handy for protecting my feet from getting banged around on rocks. I left my trail running shoes at home.

Rounding out my footwear selection are my much-maligned Crocs, which are the ultimate camp shoe. They cover your foot enough that you can walk around loose rocky areas without jabbing your foot on a rock, but they also have plenty of holes to let your feet breathe after a long day. They're also very light. My pair weigh a mere 15oz, whereas a decent pair of trail runners weigh a half pound more at 1lb 7oz. A half pound may not seem like much, but every ounce counts when you have to carry it around on your back. Crocs are also easy to put on; just step right into them and away you go. They can also be easily clipped to the outside of a pack with a carabiner, saving space inside the pack, and because of their space-age foam construction material, they don't make any noise when they swing around. Water runs right off them. Best of all, they come in very bright colors. Mine are red.

I catch a lot of flak about my Crocs, but I really don't care. I don't go into the great outdoors to look good, even though I usually do because of my rugged good looks and shapely love handles. I'm there to enjoy myself as much as possible, and the best gear helps me do that. If the best gear also happens to be reviled by some as a fashion faux pas, well, it's still the best. Deal with it.

Backpacks

I brought two backpacks to Aconcagua. My minimal ultralight pack that I use for trekking around home, and a much larger, sturdier pack.

I have had my minimalist pack for a few years. It's about 35 liters in capacity, which makes it good for a multi-day trip around home. It's big enough to fit everything I need in it, but small enough to discourage over-packing. Sometimes it is wise to consider whether a certain item will make the time you spend in camp good enough to justify its weight on your back when you are hiking, and a smaller pack encourages these evaluations. It wasn't nearly big enough to carry my gigantic warm sleeping bag or a pair of double plastic boots, though, so I had to bring a heavyweight option as well.

I am lucky in that I get to review outdoor gear in my everyday life, and it just so happened that Osprey had a pack for me to take, the Aether 70. At 70 liters it was plenty big enough to haul everything I needed to haul, and it had excellent straps and a hip belt. I've had a few pieces of Osprey gear before and I've always been impressed. My two full reviews of this pack are available at tripleblaze.com, as well as on my site at jimhodgson.com, or just Google "Osprey Aether 70 Review" and you'll find my thoughts as well as others'. Thanks, Osprey!

Underwear, Socks, and Gloves

Mark and I are both huge fans of Smartwool merino wool. I got a pair of Smartwool socks for Christmas a few years ago and loved them so much that I have, over time, collected a full suit of Smartwool garments in which to swaddle myself head to toe. It's warm, comfortable, and easy to wash. Their socks are so loved by me that I regularly give them to family and friends as Christmas gifts. They are universally praised by the recipients.

I also have a pair of Smartwool glove liners that I wore pretty much nonstop on Aconcagua. I have worn them so much now that the thumbs are threadbare. I'll have to get a new pair before I go out into the cold again, which I certainly will. They're indispensable.

For regular underwear, I'm a fan of the ExOfficio boxers. They're comfortable, easy to wash in a foreign sink, and pack down very small.

Mark and I heavily researched what gloves to bring on the trip. On Kilimanjaro, Mark wore some ski gloves he owned and was very uncomfortable. I wore my Smartwool gloves, a pair of wool gloves over those, and a pair of Gore Tex mitts over that. I was ok. Mark had to borrow another pair of gloves from one of our guides, and still spent most of the walk to the summit with hands jammed down in his pockets. We knew Aconcagua was going to be lots colder, so we wanted to really bring some heavy duty gloves. We settled on Outdoor Research Alti expedition mitts, which were designed for 8000-meter peaks. We figured since we were only going to 7000 meters, we should be fine. These suckers are expensive, but once you've had hands so cold they physically ache like crazy, not to mention experienced the shame of having to beg gear off your guide, you'll shell out for some nicer kit for the next trip.

Trekking Poles

Trekking poles were nice to have on Kilimanjaro. They were absolutely essential on Aconcagua. As many times as I fell on my ass on Aconcagua, it would have been many more had I not been using trekking poles. Even the guides use poles, although they usually carry only one. I have a pair of cheap aluminum poles, although it is possible to spend quite a bit of money on carbon versions to save weight. I'd like to have some carbon poles, but only in hopes that someone would look at them and go "Ooh, carbon fiber," which, of course, no one ever would.

Miscellaneous Essentials

Three things that proved themselves absolutely essential on Aconcagua: hand sanitizer, lip balm, and a buff. Normally I would include a packable wide brimmed hat in this list, and I did take one with me, but the force of the wind makes wearing a brimmed hat very impractical. Also, because I was always looking down at the trail to avoid falling or turning an ankle, the hat's brim didn't really protect my neck from the sun that much.

I'm not a germophobe or anything, but when I go into the outdoors I always have a small squeeze bottle of hand sanitizer in my pocket. Hikers often complain of getting sick from improperly sanitized water. I'm sure this does occasionally happen, but I'm willing to bet that many of those trail illnesses are actually a result of bathroom and kitchen conditions not being as sanitary as they are at home. Whenever I shake hands with another hiker I think to myself, "Okay, this guy probably took a crap on a tree and then wiped with a piece of bark about 20 minutes ago." I sanitize my hands just to be on the safe side. I glare at the other hiker and whisper "Unclean!" in a hoarse voice over and over while I do this.

The Aconcagua base camp staff do their best to keep the poop shacks clean using boiling water and normal cleaning products daily, but it's still a plywood shack perched over an open barrel of waste where a bunch of filthy climbers are transacting business. Some people say cleanliness is next to godliness. I'm not a terribly religious man, but cleanliness is without a doubt next to healthiness.

Right next to the hand sanitizer in my pocket is some lip balm. I never use the stuff around home, but when I go outside, especially if I'm going somewhere where it blows with the force of the Devil's own breath, I apply it regularly. Gross dried-out cracked lips are no fun at all. I don't buy any fancy kind of lip balm. On this trip I carried two tubes of generic stuff I found next to the register at my local outfitter and it worked great. Some people are crazy particular about brand, but I think the ingredients are pretty similar across the board. Having said that, the kind I bought had some spearmint essential oil, which was nice. I brush my teeth so they smell nice. My lips might as well smell nice as well, right? Get a whiff of these minty lips, people!

Also typically in my pocket on an outdoor trip is a mini Leatherman, but mine got confiscated in Santiago. Dang it. Thought I checked that.

Last, but far from least, and perhaps the number one most essential item was my buff. It is a very simple garment. It's just a stretchy tube that you pull over your head. It ends up resting around your neck most of the time, but you can also wear it like a stocking cap. It's very easy to raise and lower the level of the buff to provide more or less warmth. At frigid high altitudes, a buff and a stocking cap are my headgear of choice. You could probably use a bandanna in a similar way, but this would require a lot of knotting and re-knotting. The stretchy buff just adjusts to wherever it needs to be and hangs out there. On our summit push, I cut a hole in my buff so I could breathe through it, pulled it up over my nose, and then put my glacier goggles over it. On top of my head I put my stocking cap, then pulled my wind shell and belay jacket hoods up and put one foot in front of the other until there wasn't any mountain left to climb. Easy!

THANKS

Thanks to Owen Gaddis at SmartFlyer (smartflyer.com) for his expert travel advice and arrangement, Mitch Davis at the Gear Revival (thegearrevival.com) for crucial gear advice and outfitting, and Karin Beuerlein (karinbeuerlein.com) for her editing. Thank you Osprey Packs (ospreypacks.com) for the use of an Aether 70 backpack. Thanks to the city of Mendoza, Argentina for being so incredibly gorgeous and lovable, and thanks to plate tectonics for not making Aconcagua any taller.

Thanks to Singletracks.com and Tripleblaze.com for paying me to write humor about the outdoors. Thanks to John Hargrave, Justin Nihiser, and my family for encouraging me to keep exploring and writing.

Thanks to Dr. Patrick Segeleon, MD for his help with hemoglobin physiology and for being a fellow car guy. Thanks to the staff of the Atlanta Fulton Public Library System for being so patient.

Thanks most of all to you for reading.

JIM HODGSON

ABOUT THE AUTHOR

Jim Hodgson is an a writer who enjoys going outside. He was adopted by his parents shortly after his birth in 1974. He is a former 320lb person who has lost over 100lbs, run marathons, raced bicycles, raced cars, and completed an Ironman triathlon.

For work, he writes outdoor product reviews, travel pieces, and is even happy to write copy for businesses. He has written for Georgia Music Magazine and Creative Loafing. He is the Editor-In-Chief of the satirical Atlanta newspaper The Atlanta Banana, and often writes humorous short stories and sketches.

He occasionally performs standup comedy, and is working on a hilarious novel due out in 2014.

Find him at jimhodgson.com or on twitter at @jimhodgson.

Made in the USA
San Bernardino, CA
13 December 2013